C-3154 CAREER EXAMINATION SERIES

This is your PASSBOOK for...

Payroll Supervisor

Test Preparation Study Guide Questions & Answers

NATIONAL LEARNING CORPORATION®

National Learning Corporation

212 Michael Drive, Syosset, NY 11791
(516) 921-8888 • www.passbooks.com
E-mail: info@passbooks.com

PUBLISHED IN THE UNITED STATES OF AMERICA

COPYRIGHT NOTICE

PASSBOOK® SERIES

THE *PASSBOOK® SERIES* has been created to prepare applicants and candidates for the ultimate academic battlefield – the examination room.

At some time in our lives, each and every one of us may be required to take an examination – for validation, matriculation, admission, qualification, registration, certification, or licensure.

Based on the assumption that every applicant or candidate has met the basic formal educational standards, has taken the required number of courses, and read the necessary texts, the *PASSBOOK® SERIES* furnishes the one special preparation which may assure passing with confidence, instead of failing with insecurity. Examination questions – together with answers – are furnished as the basic vehicle for study so that the mysteries of the examination and its compounding difficulties may be eliminated or diminished by a sure method.

This book is meant to help you pass your examination provided that you qualify and are serious in your objective.

The entire field is reviewed through the huge store of content information which is succinctly presented through a provocative and challenging approach – the question-and-answer method.

A climate of success is established by furnishing the correct answers at the end of each test.

You soon learn to recognize types of questions, forms of questions, and patterns of questioning. You may even begin to anticipate expected outcomes.

You perceive that many questions are repeated or adapted so that you can gain acute insights, which may enable you to score many sure points.

You learn how to confront new questions, or types of questions, and to attack them confidently and work out the correct answers.

You note objectives and emphases, and recognize pitfalls and dangers, so that you may make positive educational adjustments.

Moreover, you are kept fully informed in relation to new concepts, methods, practices, and directions in the field.

You discover that you are actually taking the examination all the time: you are preparing for the examination by "taking" an examination, not by reading extraneous and/or supererogatory textbooks.

In short, this PASSBOOK®, used directedly, should be an important factor in helping you to pass your test.

PAYROLL SUPERVISOR

DUTIES:

Under general direction, the incumbent is responsible for all aspects of payroll processing to ensure compliance with Federal, State and local laws which involves working with departmental payroll clerks to assist in the accurate completion of payroll records. The incumbent must maintain accurate accounting records of all transactions and performs related work as necessary for the efficient fiscal functions of the department.

Incumbents of this class are responsible for overseeing, planning, coordinating, and supervising operational activities related to payroll preparation and auditing. Responsibilities involve work on payroll matters where various pay plans and differentials are in effect as well as maintaining frequent contact with various departmental sections to effectively coordinate workflow relating to payroll operations. Supervision may be exercised over a number of subordinate clerical personnel, or in departments with multiple locations, the position may act in a lead capacity, providing coordination and oversight for departmental payroll functions.

The Payroll Supervisor coordinates, directs and reviews payroll activities to ensure proper payroll processing. This includes supervision of a small staff and review, coordination and instruction of all payroll personnel resident in all departments as well as data processing personnel. The work involves update implementation, maintenance of parameter tables and similar tasks inherent with the management of a computerized payroll system. Reconciliation of the payroll is performed. This includes monitoring data input sheets and payroll data verification. Reports are generated to provide necessary information. Reconciliation to general budget ledger information is performed. Professional contact with outside agencies include retirement systems to ensure proper payment and member crediting as well as local financial institutions and State and Federal Agencies for the purpose of earnings and tax reporting. Does related duties as required.

SUBJECT OF EXAMINATION:

The written test is designed to evaluate knowledge, skills and /or abilities in the following areas:

1. **Arithmetic computation** - These questions test for the ability to use a calculator to do basic computations. Questions will involve addition, subtraction, multiplication and division. You may also be asked to calculate averages, to use percents, and to round an answer to the nearest whole number.
2. **Name and number checking** -These questions test for the ability to distinguish between sets of words, letters, and/or numbers that are almost exactly alike. Material is usually presented in two or three columns, and you will have to determine how the entry in the first column compares with the entry in the second column and possibly the third. You will be instructed to mark your answers according to a designated code provided in the directions.

3. **Office record keeping** - These questions test your ability to perform common office record keeping tasks. The test consists of two or more "sets" of questions, each set concerning a different problem. Typical record keeping problems might involve the organization or collation of data from several sources; scheduling; maintaining a record system using running balances; or completion of a table summarizing data using totals, subtotals, averages and percents.
4. **Operations with Letters and Numbers** - These questions test for skills and abilities in operations involving alphabetizing, comparing, checking and counting. The questions require you to follow the specific directions given for each question which may involve alphabetizing, comparing, checking and counting given groups of letters and/or numbers.
5. **Public contact principles and practices** - These questions test for knowledge of techniques used to interact with other people, to gather and present information, and to provide assistance, advice, and effective customer service in a courteous and professional manner. Questions will cover such topics as understanding and responding to people with diverse needs, perspectives, personalities, and levels of familiarity with agency operations, as well as acting in a way that both serves the public and reflects well on your agency.
6. **Supervision** - These questions test for knowledge of the principles and practices employed in planning, organizing, and controlling the activities of a work unit toward predetermined objectives. The concepts covered, usually in a situational question format, include such topics as assigning and reviewing work; evaluating performance; maintaining work standards; motivating and developing subordinates; implementing procedural change; increasing efficiency; and dealing with problems of absenteeism, morale, and discipline.

HOW TO TAKE A TEST

I. YOU MUST PASS AN EXAMINATION

A. WHAT EVERY CANDIDATE SHOULD KNOW

Examination applicants often ask us for help in preparing for the written test. What can I study in advance? What kinds of questions will be asked? How will the test be given? How will the papers be graded?

As an applicant for a civil service examination, you may be wondering about some of these things. Our purpose here is to suggest effective methods of advance study and to describe civil service examinations.

Your chances for success on this examination can be increased if you know how to prepare. Those "pre-examination jitters" can be reduced if you know what to expect. You can even experience an adventure in good citizenship if you know why civil service exams are given.

B. WHY ARE CIVIL SERVICE EXAMINATIONS GIVEN?

Civil service examinations are important to you in two ways. As a citizen, you want public jobs filled by employees who know how to do their work. As a job seeker, you want a fair chance to compete for that job on an equal footing with other candidates. The best-known means of accomplishing this two-fold goal is the competitive examination.

Exams are widely publicized throughout the nation. They may be administered for jobs in federal, state, city, municipal, town or village governments or agencies.

Any citizen may apply, with some limitations, such as the age or residence of applicants. Your experience and education may be reviewed to see whether you meet the requirements for the particular examination. When these requirements exist, they are reasonable and applied consistently to all applicants. Thus, a competitive examination may cause you some uneasiness now, but it is your privilege and safeguard.

C. HOW ARE CIVIL SERVICE EXAMS DEVELOPED?

Examinations are carefully written by trained technicians who are specialists in the field known as "psychological measurement," in consultation with recognized authorities in the field of work that the test will cover. These experts recommend the subject matter areas or skills to be tested; only those knowledges or skills important to your success on the job are included. The most reliable books and source materials available are used as references. Together, the experts and technicians judge the difficulty level of the questions.

Test technicians know how to phrase questions so that the problem is clearly stated. Their ethics do not permit "trick" or "catch" questions. Questions may have been tried out on sample groups, or subjected to statistical analysis, to determine their usefulness.

Written tests are often used in combination with performance tests, ratings of training and experience, and oral interviews. All of these measures combine to form the best-known means of finding the right person for the right job.

II. HOW TO PASS THE WRITTEN TEST

A. NATURE OF THE EXAMINATION

To prepare intelligently for civil service examinations, you should know how they differ from school examinations you have taken. In school you were assigned certain definite pages to read or subjects to cover. The examination questions were quite detailed and usually emphasized memory. Civil service exams, on the other hand, try to discover your present ability to perform the duties of a position, plus your potentiality to learn these duties. In other words, a civil service exam attempts to predict how successful you will be. Questions cover such a broad area that they cannot be as minute and detailed as school exam questions.

In the public service similar kinds of work, or positions, are grouped together in one "class." This process is known as *position-classification.* All the positions in a class are paid according to the salary range for that class. One class title covers all of these positions, and they are all tested by the same examination.

B. FOUR BASIC STEPS

1) Study the announcement

How, then, can you know what subjects to study? Our best answer is: "Learn as much as possible about the class of positions for which you've applied." The exam will test the knowledge, skills and abilities needed to do the work.

Your most valuable source of information about the position you want is the official exam announcement. This announcement lists the training and experience qualifications. Check these standards and apply only if you come reasonably close to meeting them.

The brief description of the position in the examination announcement offers some clues to the subjects which will be tested. Think about the job itself. Review the duties in your mind. Can you perform them, or are there some in which you are rusty? Fill in the blank spots in your preparation.

Many jurisdictions preview the written test in the exam announcement by including a section called "Knowledge and Abilities Required," "Scope of the Examination," or some similar heading. Here you will find out specifically what fields will be tested.

2) Review your own background

Once you learn in general what the position is all about, and what you need to know to do the work, ask yourself which subjects you already know fairly well and which need improvement. You may wonder whether to concentrate on improving your strong areas or on building some background in your fields of weakness. When the announcement has specified "some knowledge" or "considerable knowledge," or has used adjectives like "beginning principles of..." or "advanced ... methods," you can get a clue as to the number and difficulty of questions to be asked in any given field. More questions, and hence broader coverage, would be included for those subjects which are more important in the work. Now weigh your strengths and weaknesses against the job requirements and prepare accordingly.

3) Determine the level of the position

Another way to tell how intensively you should prepare is to understand the level of the job for which you are applying. Is it the entering level? In other words, is this the position in which beginners in a field of work are hired? Or is it an intermediate or advanced level? Sometimes this is indicated by such words as "Junior" or "Senior" in the class title. Other jurisdictions use Roman numerals to designate the level – Clerk I, Clerk II, for example. The word "Supervisor" sometimes appears in the title. If the level is not indicated by the title, check the description of duties. Will you be working under very close supervision, or will you have responsibility for independent decisions in this work?

4) Choose appropriate study materials

Now that you know the subjects to be examined and the relative amount of each subject to be covered, you can choose suitable study materials. For beginning level jobs, or even advanced ones, if you have a pronounced weakness in some aspect of your training, read a modern, standard textbook in that field. Be sure it is up to date and has general coverage. Such books are normally available at your library, and the librarian will be glad to help you locate one. For entry-level positions, questions of appropriate difficulty are chosen – neither highly advanced questions, nor those too simple. Such questions require careful thought but not advanced training.

If the position for which you are applying is technical or advanced, you will read more advanced, specialized material. If you are already familiar with the basic principles of your field, elementary textbooks would waste your time. Concentrate on advanced textbooks and technical periodicals. Think through the concepts and review difficult problems in your field.

These are all general sources. You can get more ideas on your own initiative, following these leads. For example, training manuals and publications of the government agency which employs workers in your field can be useful, particularly for technical and professional positions. A letter or visit to the government department involved may result in more specific study suggestions, and certainly will provide you with a more definite idea of the exact nature of the position you are seeking.

III. KINDS OF TESTS

Tests are used for purposes other than measuring knowledge and ability to perform specified duties. For some positions, it is equally important to test ability to make adjustments to new situations or to profit from training. In others, basic mental abilities not dependent on information are essential. Questions which test these things may not appear as pertinent to the duties of the position as those which test for knowledge and information. Yet they are often highly important parts of a fair examination. For very general questions, it is almost impossible to help you direct your study efforts. What we can do is to point out some of the more common of these general abilities needed in public service positions and describe some typical questions.

1) General information

Broad, general information has been found useful for predicting job success in some kinds of work. This is tested in a variety of ways, from vocabulary lists to questions about current events. Basic background in some field of work, such as sociology or economics, may be sampled in a group of questions. Often these are principles which have become familiar to most persons through exposure rather than through formal training. It is difficult to advise you how to study for these questions; being alert to the world around you is our best suggestion.

2) Verbal ability

An example of an ability needed in many positions is verbal or language ability. Verbal ability is, in brief, the ability to use and understand words. Vocabulary and grammar tests are typical measures of this ability. Reading comprehension or paragraph interpretation questions are common in many kinds of civil service tests. You are given a paragraph of written material and asked to find its central meaning.

3) Numerical ability

Number skills can be tested by the familiar arithmetic problem, by checking paired lists of numbers to see which are alike and which are different, or by interpreting charts and graphs. In the latter test, a graph may be printed in the test booklet which you are asked to use as the basis for answering questions.

4) Observation

A popular test for law-enforcement positions is the observation test. A picture is shown to you for several minutes, then taken away. Questions about the picture test your ability to observe both details and larger elements.

5) Following directions

In many positions in the public service, the employee must be able to carry out written instructions dependably and accurately. You may be given a chart with several columns, each column listing a variety of information. The questions require you to carry out directions involving the information given in the chart.

6) Skills and aptitudes

Performance tests effectively measure some manual skills and aptitudes. When the skill is one in which you are trained, such as typing or shorthand, you can practice. These tests are often very much like those given in business school or high school courses. For many of the other skills and aptitudes, however, no short-time preparation can be made. Skills and abilities natural to you or that you have developed throughout your lifetime are being tested.

Many of the general questions just described provide all the data needed to answer the questions and ask you to use your reasoning ability to find the answers. Your best preparation for these tests, as well as for tests of facts and ideas, is to be at your physical and mental best. You, no doubt, have your own methods of getting into an exam-taking mood and keeping "in shape." The next section lists some ideas on this subject.

IV. KINDS OF QUESTIONS

Only rarely is the "essay" question, which you answer in narrative form, used in civil service tests. Civil service tests are usually of the short-answer type. Full instructions for answering these questions will be given to you at the examination. But in case this is your first experience with short-answer questions and separate answer sheets, here is what you need to know:

1) Multiple-choice Questions

Most popular of the short-answer questions is the "multiple choice" or "best answer" question. It can be used, for example, to test for factual knowledge, ability to solve problems or judgment in meeting situations found at work.

A multiple-choice question is normally one of three types—

- It can begin with an incomplete statement followed by several possible endings. You are to find the one ending which *best* completes the statement, although some of the others may not be entirely wrong.
- It can also be a complete statement in the form of a question which is answered by choosing one of the statements listed.

- It can be in the form of a problem – again you select the best answer.

Here is an example of a multiple-choice question with a discussion which should give you some clues as to the method for choosing the right answer:

When an employee has a complaint about his assignment, the action which will *best* help him overcome his difficulty is to

A. discuss his difficulty with his coworkers
B. take the problem to the head of the organization
C. take the problem to the person who gave him the assignment
D. say nothing to anyone about his complaint

In answering this question, you should study each of the choices to find which is best. Consider choice "A" – Certainly an employee may discuss his complaint with fellow employees, but no change or improvement can result, and the complaint remains unresolved. Choice "B" is a poor choice since the head of the organization probably does not know what assignment you have been given, and taking your problem to him is known as "going over the head" of the supervisor. The supervisor, or person who made the assignment, is the person who can clarify it or correct any injustice. Choice "C" is, therefore, correct. To say nothing, as in choice "D," is unwise. Supervisors have and interest in knowing the problems employees are facing, and the employee is seeking a solution to his problem.

2) True/False Questions

The "true/false" or "right/wrong" form of question is sometimes used. Here a complete statement is given. Your job is to decide whether the statement is right or wrong.

SAMPLE: A roaming cell-phone call to a nearby city costs less than a non-roaming call to a distant city.

This statement is wrong, or false, since roaming calls are more expensive.

This is not a complete list of all possible question forms, although most of the others are variations of these common types. You will always get complete directions for answering questions. Be sure you understand *how* to mark your answers – ask questions until you do.

V. RECORDING YOUR ANSWERS

Computer terminals are used more and more today for many different kinds of exams.

For an examination with very few applicants, you may be told to record your answers in the test booklet itself. Separate answer sheets are much more common. If this separate answer sheet is to be scored by machine – and this is often the case – it is highly important that you mark your answers correctly in order to get credit.

An electronic scoring machine is often used in civil service offices because of the speed with which papers can be scored. Machine-scored answer sheets must be marked with a pencil, which will be given to you. This pencil has a high graphite content which responds to the electronic scoring machine. As a matter of fact, stray dots may register as answers, so do not let your pencil rest on the answer sheet while you are pondering the correct answer. Also, if your pencil lead breaks or is otherwise defective, ask for another.

Since the answer sheet will be dropped in a slot in the scoring machine, be careful not to bend the corners or get the paper crumpled.

The answer sheet normally has five vertical columns of numbers, with 30 numbers to a column. These numbers correspond to the question numbers in your test booklet. After each number, going across the page are four or five pairs of dotted lines. These short dotted lines have small letters or numbers above them. The first two pairs may also have a "T" or "F" above the letters. This indicates that the first two pairs only are to be used if the questions are of the true-false type. If the questions are multiple choice, disregard the "T" and "F" and pay attention only to the small letters or numbers.

Answer your questions in the manner of the sample that follows:

32. The largest city in the United States is
    A. Washington, D.C.
    B. New York City
    C. Chicago
    D. Detroit
    E. San Francisco

1) Choose the answer you think is best. (New York City is the largest, so "B" is correct.)
2) Find the row of dotted lines numbered the same as the question you are answering. (Find row number 32)
3) Find the pair of dotted lines corresponding to the answer. (Find the pair of lines under the mark "B.")
4) Make a solid black mark between the dotted lines.

VI. BEFORE THE TEST

Common sense will help you find procedures to follow to get ready for an examination. Too many of us, however, overlook these sensible measures. Indeed, nervousness and fatigue have been found to be the most serious reasons why applicants fail to do their best on civil service tests. Here is a list of reminders:

- Begin your preparation early – Don't wait until the last minute to go scurrying around for books and materials or to find out what the position is all about.
- Prepare continuously – An hour a night for a week is better than an all-night cram session. This has been definitely established. What is more, a night a week for a month will return better dividends than crowding your study into a shorter period of time.
- Locate the place of the exam – You have been sent a notice telling you when and where to report for the examination. If the location is in a different town or otherwise unfamiliar to you, it would be well to inquire the best route and learn something about the building.
- Relax the night before the test – Allow your mind to rest. Do not study at all that night. Plan some mild recreation or diversion; then go to bed early and get a good night's sleep.
- Get up early enough to make a leisurely trip to the place for the test – This way unforeseen events, traffic snarls, unfamiliar buildings, etc. will not upset you.
- Dress comfortably – A written test is not a fashion show. You will be known by number and not by name, so wear something comfortable.

- Leave excess paraphernalia at home – Shopping bags and odd bundles will get in your way. You need bring only the items mentioned in the official notice you received; usually everything you need is provided. Do not bring reference books to the exam. They will only confuse those last minutes and be taken away from you when in the test room.
- Arrive somewhat ahead of time – If because of transportation schedules you must get there very early, bring a newspaper or magazine to take your mind off yourself while waiting.
- Locate the examination room – When you have found the proper room, you will be directed to the seat or part of the room where you will sit. Sometimes you are given a sheet of instructions to read while you are waiting. Do not fill out any forms until you are told to do so; just read them and be prepared.
- Relax and prepare to listen to the instructions
- If you have any physical problem that may keep you from doing your best, be sure to tell the test administrator. If you are sick or in poor health, you really cannot do your best on the exam. You can come back and take the test some other time.

VII. AT THE TEST

The day of the test is here and you have the test booklet in your hand. The temptation to get going is very strong. Caution! There is more to success than knowing the right answers. You must know how to identify your papers and understand variations in the type of short-answer question used in this particular examination. Follow these suggestions for maximum results from your efforts:

1) Cooperate with the monitor

The test administrator has a duty to create a situation in which you can be as much at ease as possible. He will give instructions, tell you when to begin, check to see that you are marking your answer sheet correctly, and so on. He is not there to guard you, although he will see that your competitors do not take unfair advantage. He wants to help you do your best.

2) Listen to all instructions

Don't jump the gun! Wait until you understand all directions. In most civil service tests you get more time than you need to answer the questions. So don't be in a hurry. Read each word of instructions until you clearly understand the meaning. Study the examples, listen to all announcements and follow directions. Ask questions if you do not understand what to do.

3) Identify your papers

Civil service exams are usually identified by number only. You will be assigned a number; you must not put your name on your test papers. Be sure to copy your number correctly. Since more than one exam may be given, copy your exact examination title.

4) Plan your time

Unless you are told that a test is a "speed" or "rate of work" test, speed itself is usually not important. Time enough to answer all the questions will be provided, but this does not mean that you have all day. An overall time limit has been set. Divide the total time (in minutes) by the number of questions to determine the approximate time you have for each question.

5) Do not linger over difficult questions

If you come across a difficult question, mark it with a paper clip (useful to have along) and come back to it when you have been through the booklet. One caution if you do this – be sure to skip a number on your answer sheet as well. Check often to be sure that you have not lost your place and that you are marking in the row numbered the same as the question you are answering.

6) Read the questions

Be sure you know what the question asks! Many capable people are unsuccessful because they failed to *read* the questions correctly.

7) Answer all questions

Unless you have been instructed that a penalty will be deducted for incorrect answers, it is better to guess than to omit a question.

8) Speed tests

It is often better NOT to guess on speed tests. It has been found that on timed tests people are tempted to spend the last few seconds before time is called in marking answers at random – without even reading them – in the hope of picking up a few extra points. To discourage this practice, the instructions may warn you that your score will be "corrected" for guessing. That is, a penalty will be applied. The incorrect answers will be deducted from the correct ones, or some other penalty formula will be used.

9) Review your answers

If you finish before time is called, go back to the questions you guessed or omitted to give them further thought. Review other answers if you have time.

10) Return your test materials

If you are ready to leave before others have finished or time is called, take ALL your materials to the monitor and leave quietly. Never take any test material with you. The monitor can discover whose papers are not complete, and taking a test booklet may be grounds for disqualification.

VIII. EXAMINATION TECHNIQUES

1) Read the general instructions carefully. These are usually printed on the first page of the exam booklet. As a rule, these instructions refer to the timing of the examination; the fact that you should not start work until the signal and must stop work at a signal, etc. If there are any *special* instructions, such as a choice of questions to be answered, make sure that you note this instruction carefully.

2) When you are ready to start work on the examination, that is as soon as the signal has been given, read the instructions to each question booklet, underline any key words or phrases, such as *least, best, outline, describe* and the like. In this way you will tend to answer as requested rather than discover on reviewing your paper that you *listed without describing*, that you selected the *worst* choice rather than the *best* choice, etc.

3) If the examination is of the objective or multiple-choice type – that is, each question will also give a series of possible answers: A, B, C or D, and you are called upon to select the best answer and write the letter next to that answer on your answer paper – it is advisable to start answering each question in turn. There may be anywhere from 50 to 100 such questions in the three or four hours allotted and you can see how much time would be taken if you read through all the questions before beginning to answer any. Furthermore, if you come across a question or group of questions which you know would be difficult to answer, it would undoubtedly affect your handling of all the other questions.

4) If the examination is of the essay type and contains but a few questions, it is a moot point as to whether you should read all the questions before starting to answer any one. Of course, if you are given a choice – say five out of seven and the like – then it is essential to read all the questions so you can eliminate the two that are most difficult. If, however, you are asked to answer all the questions, there may be danger in trying to answer the easiest one first because you may find that you will spend too much time on it. The best technique is to answer the first question, then proceed to the second, etc.

5) Time your answers. Before the exam begins, write down the time it started, then add the time allowed for the examination and write down the time it must be completed, then divide the time available somewhat as follows:
   - If 3-1/2 hours are allowed, that would be 210 minutes. If you have 80 objective-type questions, that would be an average of 2-1/2 minutes per question. Allow yourself no more than 2 minutes per question, or a total of 160 minutes, which will permit about 50 minutes to review.
   - If for the time allotment of 210 minutes there are 7 essay questions to answer, that would average about 30 minutes a question. Give yourself only 25 minutes per question so that you have about 35 minutes to review.

6) The most important instruction is to *read each question* and make sure you know what is wanted. The second most important instruction is to *time yourself properly* so that you answer every question. The third most important instruction is to *answer every question*. Guess if you have to but include something for each question. Remember that you will receive no credit for a blank and will probably receive some credit if you write something in answer to an essay question. If you guess a letter – say "B" for a multiple-choice question – you may have guessed right. If you leave a blank as an answer to a multiple-choice question, the examiners may respect your feelings but it will not add a point to your score. Some exams may penalize you for wrong answers, so in such cases *only*, you may not want to guess unless you have some basis for your answer.

7) Suggestions
   a. Objective-type questions
      1. Examine the question booklet for proper sequence of pages and questions
      2. Read all instructions carefully
      3. Skip any question which seems too difficult; return to it after all other questions have been answered
      4. Apportion your time properly; do not spend too much time on any single question or group of questions

5. Note and underline key words – *all, most, fewest, least, best, worst, same, opposite,* etc.
6. Pay particular attention to negatives
7. Note unusual option, e.g., unduly long, short, complex, different or similar in content to the body of the question
8. Observe the use of "hedging" words – *probably, may, most likely,* etc.
9. Make sure that your answer is put next to the same number as the question
10. Do not second-guess unless you have good reason to believe the second answer is definitely more correct
11. Cross out original answer if you decide another answer is more accurate; do not erase until you are ready to hand your paper in
12. Answer all questions; guess unless instructed otherwise
13. Leave time for review

b. Essay questions
1. Read each question carefully
2. Determine exactly what is wanted. Underline key words or phrases.
3. Decide on outline or paragraph answer
4. Include many different points and elements unless asked to develop any one or two points or elements
5. Show impartiality by giving pros and cons unless directed to select one side only
6. Make and write down any assumptions you find necessary to answer the questions
7. Watch your English, grammar, punctuation and choice of words
8. Time your answers; don't crowd material

8) Answering the essay question

Most essay questions can be answered by framing the specific response around several key words or ideas. Here are a few such key words or ideas:

M's: manpower, materials, methods, money, management
P's: purpose, program, policy, plan, procedure, practice, problems, pitfalls, personnel, public relations

a. Six basic steps in handling problems:
1. Preliminary plan and background development
2. Collect information, data and facts
3. Analyze and interpret information, data and facts
4. Analyze and develop solutions as well as make recommendations
5. Prepare report and sell recommendations
6. Install recommendations and follow up effectiveness

b. Pitfalls to avoid
1. *Taking things for granted* – A statement of the situation does not necessarily imply that each of the elements is necessarily true; for example, a complaint may be invalid and biased so that all that can be taken for granted is that a complaint has been registered

2. *Considering only one side of a situation* – Wherever possible, indicate several alternatives and then point out the reasons you selected the best one
3. *Failing to indicate follow up* – Whenever your answer indicates action on your part, make certain that you will take proper follow-up action to see how successful your recommendations, procedures or actions turn out to be
4. *Taking too long in answering any single question* – Remember to time your answers properly

IX. AFTER THE TEST

Scoring procedures differ in detail among civil service jurisdictions although the general principles are the same. Whether the papers are hand-scored or graded by machine we have described, they are nearly always graded by number. That is, the person who marks the paper knows only the number – never the name – of the applicant. Not until all the papers have been graded will they be matched with names. If other tests, such as training and experience or oral interview ratings have been given, scores will be combined. Different parts of the examination usually have different weights. For example, the written test might count 60 percent of the final grade, and a rating of training and experience 40 percent. In many jurisdictions, veterans will have a certain number of points added to their grades.

After the final grade has been determined, the names are placed in grade order and an eligible list is established. There are various methods for resolving ties between those who get the same final grade – probably the most common is to place first the name of the person whose application was received first. Job offers are made from the eligible list in the order the names appear on it. You will be notified of your grade and your rank as soon as all these computations have been made. This will be done as rapidly as possible.

People who are found to meet the requirements in the announcement are called "eligibles." Their names are put on a list of eligible candidates. An eligible's chances of getting a job depend on how high he stands on this list and how fast agencies are filling jobs from the list.

When a job is to be filled from a list of eligibles, the agency asks for the names of people on the list of eligibles for that job. When the civil service commission receives this request, it sends to the agency the names of the three people highest on this list. Or, if the job to be filled has specialized requirements, the office sends the agency the names of the top three persons who meet these requirements from the general list.

The appointing officer makes a choice from among the three people whose names were sent to him. If the selected person accepts the appointment, the names of the others are put back on the list to be considered for future openings.

That is the rule in hiring from all kinds of eligible lists, whether they are for typist, carpenter, chemist, or something else. For every vacancy, the appointing officer has his choice of any one of the top three eligibles on the list. This explains why the person whose name is on top of the list sometimes does not get an appointment when some of the persons lower on the list do. If the appointing officer chooses the second or third eligible, the No. 1 eligible does not get a job at once, but stays on the list until he is appointed or the list is terminated.

X. HOW TO PASS THE INTERVIEW TEST

The examination for which you applied requires an oral interview test. You have already taken the written test and you are now being called for the interview test – the final part of the formal examination.

You may think that it is not possible to prepare for an interview test and that there are no procedures to follow during an interview. Our purpose is to point out some things you can do in advance that will help you and some good rules to follow and pitfalls to avoid while you are being interviewed.

What is an interview supposed to test?

The written examination is designed to test the technical knowledge and competence of the candidate; the oral is designed to evaluate intangible qualities, not readily measured otherwise, and to establish a list showing the relative fitness of each candidate – as measured against his competitors – for the position sought. Scoring is not on the basis of "right" and "wrong," but on a sliding scale of values ranging from "not passable" to "outstanding." As a matter of fact, it is possible to achieve a relatively low score without a single "incorrect" answer because of evident weakness in the qualities being measured.

Occasionally, an examination may consist entirely of an oral test – either an individual or a group oral. In such cases, information is sought concerning the technical knowledges and abilities of the candidate, since there has been no written examination for this purpose. More commonly, however, an oral test is used to supplement a written examination.

Who conducts interviews?

The composition of oral boards varies among different jurisdictions. In nearly all, a representative of the personnel department serves as chairman. One of the members of the board may be a representative of the department in which the candidate would work. In some cases, "outside experts" are used, and, frequently, a businessman or some other representative of the general public is asked to serve. Labor and management or other special groups may be represented. The aim is to secure the services of experts in the appropriate field.

However the board is composed, it is a good idea (and not at all improper or unethical) to ascertain in advance of the interview who the members are and what groups they represent. When you are introduced to them, you will have some idea of their backgrounds and interests, and at least you will not stutter and stammer over their names.

What should be done before the interview?

While knowledge about the board members is useful and takes some of the surprise element out of the interview, there is other preparation which is more substantive. It *is* possible to prepare for an oral interview – in several ways:

1) Keep a copy of your application and review it carefully before the interview

This may be the only document before the oral board, and the starting point of the interview. Know what education and experience you have listed there, and the sequence and dates of all of it. Sometimes the board will ask you to review the highlights of your experience for them; you should not have to hem and haw doing it.

2) Study the class specification and the examination announcement

Usually, the oral board has one or both of these to guide them. The qualities, characteristics or knowledges required by the position sought are stated in these documents. They offer valuable clues as to the nature of the oral interview. For example, if the job involves supervisory responsibilities, the announcement will usually indicate that knowledge of modern supervisory methods and the qualifications of the candidate as a supervisor will be tested. If so, you can expect such questions, frequently in the form of a hypothetical situation which you are expected to solve. NEVER go into an oral without knowledge of the duties and responsibilities of the job you seek.

3) Think through each qualification required

Try to visualize the kind of questions you would ask if you were a board member. How well could you answer them? Try especially to appraise your own knowledge and background in each area, *measured against the job sought*, and identify any areas in which you are weak. Be critical and realistic – do not flatter yourself.

4) Do some general reading in areas in which you feel you may be weak

For example, if the job involves supervision and your past experience has NOT, some general reading in supervisory methods and practices, particularly in the field of human relations, might be useful. Do NOT study agency procedures or detailed manuals. The oral board will be testing your understanding and capacity, not your memory.

5) Get a good night's sleep and watch your general health and mental attitude

You will want a clear head at the interview. Take care of a cold or any other minor ailment, and of course, no hangovers.

What should be done on the day of the interview?

Now comes the day of the interview itself. Give yourself plenty of time to get there. Plan to arrive somewhat ahead of the scheduled time, particularly if your appointment is in the fore part of the day. If a previous candidate fails to appear, the board might be ready for you a bit early. By early afternoon an oral board is almost invariably behind schedule if there are many candidates, and you may have to wait. Take along a book or magazine to read, or your application to review, but leave any extraneous material in the waiting room when you go in for your interview. In any event, relax and compose yourself.

The matter of dress is important. The board is forming impressions about you – from your experience, your manners, your attitude, and your appearance. Give your personal appearance careful attention. Dress your best, but not your flashiest. Choose conservative, appropriate clothing, and be sure it is immaculate. This is a business interview, and your appearance should indicate that you regard it as such. Besides, being well groomed and properly dressed will help boost your confidence.

Sooner or later, someone will call your name and escort you into the interview room. *This is it.* From here on you are on your own. It is too late for any more preparation. But remember, you asked for this opportunity to prove your fitness, and you are here because your request was granted.

What happens when you go in?

The usual sequence of events will be as follows: The clerk (who is often the board stenographer) will introduce you to the chairman of the oral board, who will introduce you to the other members of the board. Acknowledge the introductions before you sit down. Do not be surprised if you find a microphone facing you or a stenotypist sitting by. Oral interviews are usually recorded in the event of an appeal or other review.

Usually the chairman of the board will open the interview by reviewing the highlights of your education and work experience from your application – primarily for the benefit of the other members of the board, as well as to get the material into the record. Do not interrupt or comment unless there is an error or significant misinterpretation; if that is the case, do not hesitate. But do not quibble about insignificant matters. Also, he will usually ask you some question about your education, experience or your present job – partly to get you to start talking and to establish the interviewing "rapport." He may start the actual questioning, or turn it over to one of the other members. Frequently, each member undertakes the questioning on a particular area, one in which he is perhaps most competent, so you can expect each member to participate in the examination. Because time is limited, you may also expect some rather abrupt switches in the direction the questioning takes, so do not be upset by it. Normally, a board member will not pursue a single line of questioning unless he discovers a particular strength or weakness.

After each member has participated, the chairman will usually ask whether any member has any further questions, then will ask you if you have anything you wish to add. Unless you are expecting this question, it may floor you. Worse, it may start you off on an extended, extemporaneous speech. The board is not usually seeking more information. The question is principally to offer you a last opportunity to present further qualifications or to indicate that you have nothing to add. So, if you feel that a significant qualification or characteristic has been overlooked, it is proper to point it out in a sentence or so. Do not compliment the board on the thoroughness of their examination – they have been sketchy, and you know it. If you wish, merely say, "No thank you, I have nothing further to add." This is a point where you can "talk yourself out" of a good impression or fail to present an important bit of information. Remember, *you close the interview yourself.*

The chairman will then say, "That is all, Mr. ______, thank you." Do not be startled; the interview is over, and quicker than you think. Thank him, gather your belongings and take your leave. Save your sigh of relief for the other side of the door.

How to put your best foot forward

Throughout this entire process, you may feel that the board individually and collectively is trying to pierce your defenses, seek out your hidden weaknesses and embarrass and confuse you. Actually, this is not true. They are obliged to make an appraisal of your qualifications for the job you are seeking, and they want to see you in your best light. Remember, they must interview all candidates and a non-cooperative candidate may become a failure in spite of their best efforts to bring out his qualifications. Here are 15 suggestions that will help you:

1) Be natural – Keep your attitude confident, not cocky

If you are not confident that you can do the job, do not expect the board to be. Do not apologize for your weaknesses, try to bring out your strong points. The board is interested in a positive, not negative, presentation. Cockiness will antagonize any board member and make him wonder if you are covering up a weakness by a false show of strength.

2) Get comfortable, but don't lounge or sprawl

Sit erectly but not stiffly. A careless posture may lead the board to conclude that you are careless in other things, or at least that you are not impressed by the importance of the occasion. Either conclusion is natural, even if incorrect. Do not fuss with your clothing, a pencil or an ashtray. Your hands may occasionally be useful to emphasize a point; do not let them become a point of distraction.

3) Do not wisecrack or make small talk

This is a serious situation, and your attitude should show that you consider it as such. Further, the time of the board is limited – they do not want to waste it, and neither should you.

4) Do not exaggerate your experience or abilities

In the first place, from information in the application or other interviews and sources, the board may know more about you than you think. Secondly, you probably will not get away with it. An experienced board is rather adept at spotting such a situation, so do not take the chance.

5) If you know a board member, do not make a point of it, yet do not hide it

Certainly you are not fooling him, and probably not the other members of the board. Do not try to take advantage of your acquaintanceship – it will probably do you little good.

6) Do not dominate the interview

Let the board do that. They will give you the clues – do not assume that you have to do all the talking. Realize that the board has a number of questions to ask you, and do not try to take up all the interview time by showing off your extensive knowledge of the answer to the first one.

7) Be attentive

You only have 20 minutes or so, and you should keep your attention at its sharpest throughout. When a member is addressing a problem or question to you, give him your undivided attention. Address your reply principally to him, but do not exclude the other board members.

8) Do not interrupt

A board member may be stating a problem for you to analyze. He will ask you a question when the time comes. Let him state the problem, and wait for the question.

9) Make sure you understand the question

Do not try to answer until you are sure what the question is. If it is not clear, restate it in your own words or ask the board member to clarify it for you. However, do not haggle about minor elements.

10) Reply promptly but not hastily

A common entry on oral board rating sheets is "candidate responded readily," or "candidate hesitated in replies." Respond as promptly and quickly as you can, but do not jump to a hasty, ill-considered answer.

11) Do not be peremptory in your answers

A brief answer is proper – but do not fire your answer back. That is a losing game from your point of view. The board member can probably ask questions much faster than you can answer them.

12) Do not try to create the answer you think the board member wants

He is interested in what kind of mind you have and how it works – not in playing games. Furthermore, he can usually spot this practice and will actually grade you down on it.

13) Do not switch sides in your reply merely to agree with a board member

Frequently, a member will take a contrary position merely to draw you out and to see if you are willing and able to defend your point of view. Do not start a debate, yet do not surrender a good position. If a position is worth taking, it is worth defending.

14) Do not be afraid to admit an error in judgment if you are shown to be wrong

The board knows that you are forced to reply without any opportunity for careful consideration. Your answer may be demonstrably wrong. If so, admit it and get on with the interview.

15) Do not dwell at length on your present job

The opening question may relate to your present assignment. Answer the question but do not go into an extended discussion. You are being examined for a *new* job, not your present one. As a matter of fact, try to phrase ALL your answers in terms of the job for which you are being examined.

Basis of Rating

Probably you will forget most of these "do's" and "don'ts" when you walk into the oral interview room. Even remembering them all will not ensure you a passing grade. Perhaps you did not have the qualifications in the first place. But remembering them will help you to put your best foot forward, without treading on the toes of the board members.

Rumor and popular opinion to the contrary notwithstanding, an oral board wants you to make the best appearance possible. They know you are under pressure – but they also want to see how you respond to it as a guide to what your reaction would be under the pressures of the job you seek. They will be influenced by the degree of poise you display, the personal traits you show and the manner in which you respond.

ABOUT THIS BOOK

This book contains tests divided into Examination Sections. Go through each test, answering every question in the margin. We have also attached a sample answer sheet at the back of the book that can be removed and used. At the end of each test look at the answer key and check your answers. On the ones you got wrong, look at the right answer choice and learn. Do not fill in the answers first. Do not memorize the questions and answers, but understand the answer and principles involved. On your test, the questions will likely be different from the samples. Questions are changed and new ones added. If you understand these past questions you should have success with any changes that arise. Tests may consist of several types of questions. We have additional books on each subject should more study be advisable or necessary for you. Finally, the more you study, the better prepared you will be. This book is intended to be the last thing you study before you walk into the examination room. Prior study of relevant texts is also recommended. NLC publishes some of these in our Fundamental Series. Knowledge and good sense are important factors in passing your exam. Good luck also helps. So now study this Passbook, absorb the material contained within and take that knowledge into the examination. Then do your best to pass that exam.

EXAMINATION SECTION

EXAMINATION SECTION
TEST 1

DIRECTIONS: Each question or incomplete statement is followed by several suggested answers or completions. Select the one that BEST answers the question or completes the statement. *PRINT THE LETTER OF THE CORRECT ANSWER IN THE SPACE AT THE RIGHT.*

1. The processing of payroll changes and the preparation of salary checks is done by the 1.____

   A. agency payroll unit
   B. Department of Audit and Control
   C. Department of Civil Service
   D. Office of General Services

2. Of the following, a *special payroll* 2.____

   A. is prepared during the period in which the employee is actually earning the money
   B. would need the approval of the Office of General Services
   C. would involve temporary employees
   D. would not be processed by a computer

3. Form PR-75 would be used to request 3.____

   A. a change in an employee's name
   B. overtime pay for a unit
   C. a job audit
   D. a reclassification for an employee

4. In setting due dates, DAY 14 of the payroll period in state agencies is 4.____

   A. Friday
   B. Thursday
   C. Wednesday
   D. Tuesday

5. In filling out a PR-75, if an employee _____, it would require a Group II classification. 5.____

   A. retires
   B. works overtime
   C. is reclassified
   D. receives a raise over $1,500 annually

6. In filling out a PR-75, if an employee _____, it would require a Group I classification. 6.____

   A. retires
   B. works overtime
   C. successfully completes a probationary period
   D. takes military leave without pay

7. Of the following, which deduction would NOT be directly handled by most agency payroll units? 7.____

   A. Credit union deductions
   B. Fixed federal tax
   C. Federated funds
   D. State health insurance

8. If, after percentage deductions, the employee's salary is insufficient to cover all fixed deductions, which of the following deductions should be eliminated before the others? 8.____

A. Bonds
B. Credit union
C. Taxable maintenance
D. Social Security adjustment

9. A reallocation is 9.____

A. a change in an existing title
B. a change of status from one classification to the next
C. another term for transfer of an employee
D. a change in the grade of an existing title with no change in the title

10. An employee's annual salary is $23,600. The biweekly factor based on a 365-day year is .038356. 10.____
The employee's biweekly rate would be

A. $885.90 B. $905.20 C. $615.28 D. $963.10

11. An employee's annual salary is $25,000. The employee is paid for 8 days in a biweekly period of 10 hour days for a 366-day year. The biweekly factor is .038251, and the work day factor is .125. 11.____
What is the employee's work day rate?

A. $111.56 B. $956 C. $119.54 D. $116.28

12. An employee has an annual salary of $13,850. There is a lump sum payment owed to the employee for accured credits totaling 6 days. The biweekly factor is .038356, and the work day rate is .10. 12.____
The employee should receive a lump sum payment of

A. $531.23 B. $318.74 C. $391.14 D. $481.15

13. An employee has an annual salary of $15,860. The biweekly factor is .048761, and the work day rate is .125. The employee's work day rate would be 13.____

A. $96.73 B. $89.45 C. $98.64 D. $92.55

14. An employee's biweekly rate is $567.67. The hourly overtime rate is paid by the following formula: Annual Salary x .00075. The biweekly factor is .038356. 14.____
If the employee works 8 hours of overtime, how much money will he have earned for the overtime?

A. $148.00 B. $42.58 C. $88.80 D. $96.50

15. An employee is paid on a biweekly basis over 21 biweekly pay periods. The employee's annual salary is $19,500. The biweekly factor is .047619, and the calendar day factor is .0714286. 15.____
Approximately what is her calendar day rate?

A. $66.33 B. $92.86 C. $78.54 D. $73.58

KEY (CORRECT ANSWERS)

1. B
2. C
3. A
4. C
5. A
6. C
7. D
8. A
9. D
10. B
11. C
12. B
13. A
14. C
15. A

EXAMINATION SECTION
TEST 1

DIRECTIONS: Each question or incomplete statement is followed by several suggested answers or completions. Select the one that BEST answers the question or completes the statement. *PRINT THE LETTER OF THE CORRECT ANSWER IN THE SPACE AT THE RIGHT.*

Questions 1-12.

DIRECTIONS: Questions 1 through 12 refer to the following information.

At the Supreme Plastic Company, located in Detroit, employees are paid bi-weekly. Their paychecks are calculated on the following deductions from their gross pay:

a. Federal and State tax combined is 14%
b. City tax of 3%, only for Detroit residents
c. Union dues for union members only. The union dues are calculated as follows: 1.5% of an employee's gross pay or $15, whichever is smaller
d. Medical coverage, which is calculated as follows: 2% of gross pay for employees under the age of 30, and 3.5% of gross pay for employees 30 years of age or older.

1. Charlie's gross pay per paycheck is $840. He lives outside Detroit, is not a union member, and is 36 years old. What is his net pay? 1.____

A. $680.40 B. $693.00 C. $705.60 D. $718.20 E. $730.80

2. Diane's gross pay per paycheck is $920. She lives in Detroit, is not a union member, and is 29 years old. What is her net pay? 2.____

A. $782.00 B. $772.80 C. $763.60 D. $754.40 E. $745.20

3. Barney's gross pay per paycheck is $1030. He lives outside Detroit, is a union member, and is 25 years old. What is his net pay? 3.____

A. $850.20 B. $857.70 C. $865.20 D. $872.70 E. $880.20

4. Vanessa's gross pay per paycheck is $980. She lives in Detroit, is a union member, and is 40 years old. What is her net pay? 4.____

A. $749.70 B. $757.05 C. $764.40 D. $771.75 E. $779.10

5. Fred's gross pay per paycheck is $750. He lives in Detroit, is a union member, and is 30 years old. What is his net pay? 5.____

A. $607.50 B. $596.25 C. $585.00 D. $573.75 E. $562.50

6. Christine lives outside Detroit, is not a union member, and is 23 years old. Her net pay per paycheck is $567.00. What is her gross pay? 6.____

A. $662.50 B. $675.00 C. $687.50 D. $700.00 E. $712.50

7. Marie lives in Detroit, is not a union member, and is 33 years old. Her net pay per paycheck is $890.40. 7.___
What is her gross pay?

A. $1060.00 B. $1080.00 C. $1100.00
D. $1120.00 E. $1140.00

8. Todd lives outside Detroit, is a union member, and is 45 years old. His net pay per paycheck is $607.82. 8.___
What is his gross pay?

A. $779.60 B. $772.30 C. $765.00 D. $757.70 E. $750.40

9. Priscilla lives in Detroit, is a union member, and is 27 years old. Her net pay per paycheck is $981.46. 9.___
What is her gross pay?

A. $1246.80 B. $1238.50 C. $1230.20
D. $1221.90 E. $1213.60

10. During the first two-week pay period in May, Floyd was a Detroit resident and not a union member. As of the second two-week pay period in May, he moved out of Detroit and joined the company union. 10.___
If his gross pay per paycheck remained at $1300, how much was the *increase* in net pay?

A. $15.00 B. $19.50 C. $24.00 D. $28.50 E. $33.00

11. During the first two-week pay period in July, Paula was not a Detroit resident, but was a union member. As of the second two-week pay period in July, she moved to Detroit and left the company union. 11.___
If her gross pay per paycheck remained at $880, how much was the *decrease* in net pay?

A. $9.60 B. $10.50 C. $11.40 D. $12.30 E. $13.20

12. Roger is a 50-year-old employee. During the first two-week pay period in August, he carried medical insurance. Due to financial hardship, he was allowed to drop this coverage as of the second two-week pay period. The net pay on his second paycheck was $18.92 higher than that of his first paycheck. 12.___
What is his gross pay?

A. $524.10 B. $529.60 C. $535.10 D. $540.60 E. $546.10

Questions 13-25.

DIRECTIONS: Questions 13 through 25 refer to the following information.

At the Lucky Star Restaurant, employees are paid weekly. Their paychecks are calculated on the following deductions from their gross pay (salary earnings):

a. Federal and State tax combined is applied to salary earnings only (not including tips) in the following manner: 12% of salary up to and including a weekly salary of $400, plus 10% of any salary in excess of $400
b. Tax on tips. This is calculated on <u>the larger of</u> $3 or 2% of tips collected.

c. Medical coverage, which is optional. The amount deducted is as shown in this chart:

Employee's Age (Yrs)	Employee's Years of Service		
	Less Than 1 Year	1-5 Years	Over 5 Years
18-30	$5	$4	$3
31-40	$9	$7	$5
Over 40	$13	$10	$7

NOTE: Net pay will include the tips earned, if the person involved did earn tips.

13. Frank's gross pay per paycheck is $380, including tips. In a particular week, he receives $50 in tips. 13.____
If he has no medical coverage, what is his net pay?

A. $387.40 B. $385.40 C. $383.40 D. $381.40 E. $379.40

14. Gina's gross pay per paycheck is $460, excluding tips. In a particular week, she receives $70 in tips. 14.____
If she has no medical coverage, what is her net pay?

A. $461.00 B. $467.00 C. $473.00 D. $479.00 E. $485.00

15. Cliff's gross pay per paycheck is $510, excluding tips. In a particular week, he receives $180 in tips. 15.____
If he has no medical coverage, what is his net pay?

A. $627.40 B. $638.00 C. $648.60 D. $659.20 E. $669.80

16. Diane's gross pay per paycheck is $350, excluding tips. In a particular week, she receives $200 in tips. 16.____
If she has no medical coverage, what is her net pay?

A. $506.00 B. $505.50 C. $505.00 D. $504.50 E. $504.00

17. Jean is a part-time cashier, earning a weekly salary of $320. She receives no tips, but does carry medical coverage. 17.____
If she is 23 years old and has 4 years of service, what is her net pay?

A. $275.60 B. $277.60 C. $279.60 D. $281.60 E. $283.60

18. Pete is a part-time cook, earning a weekly salary of $440. He receives no tips, but does carry medical coverage. 18.____
If he is 42 years old and has 8 years of service, what is his net pay?

A. $377.80 B. $378.60 C. $379.40 D. $380.20 E. $381.00

19. Melissa is a waitress, earning a weekly salary of $560, excluding tips. During one week, she receives $130 in tips. 19.____
If she has medical coverage, is 36 years old, and has 5 years of service, what is her net pay?

A. $613.00 B. $616.00 C. $619.00 D. $622.00 E. $625.00

20. Henry is a part-time waiter, earning a weekly salary of $350, excluding tips. During one week, he receives $90 in tips. 20.____
If he has medical coverage, is 32 years old, and has 7 months of service, what is his net pay?

A. $386.00 B. $388.00 C. $390.00 D. $392.00 E. $394.00

21. During the first week of November, Roseanne was a waitress, earning a weekly salary of $570, plus $140 in tips. During the second week of November, her weekly salary was increased by 6% and her tips rose by 10%. What was her total net pay for these two weeks? (Assume no medical coverage for either week.) 21.____

A. $1311.90 B. $1317.50 C. $1323.10
D. $1328.70 E. $1334.30

22. During the first week of October, Don was a waiter, earning a weekly salary of $610, plus $100 in tips. He had no medical coverage at that time. During the second week of October, he was promoted to an Assistant Manager with a weekly salary of $800 and no tips. He also carried medical coverage. During that time frame, he had 4 years of service and was 52 years old. 22.____
What was his total net pay for these weeks?

A. $1320.00 B. $1325.00 C. $1330.00
D. $1335.00 E. $1340.00

23. Arlene is a waitress, 46 years old, with 10 months of service. During one particular week, she had $50 in tips and net pay of $305.04. 23.____
If she has medical coverage, what is her gross pay, excluding tips?

A. $296.00 B. $302.00 C. $308.00 D. $314.00 E. $320.00

24. Francine is the restaurant's bookkeeper. She is 39 years old with 10 years of service. She carries medical coverage and her weekly salary includes no tips. 24.____
If her net pay per week is $869.45, what is her gross pay?

A. $980.50 B. $978.10 C. $975.70 D. $973.30 E. $970.90

25. Ray is the chief waiter. He is 60 years old with 20 years of service. He carries medical coverage and his gross weekly salary, excluding tips, is $750. Assuming his weekly tips exceed $150, if his net pay (including salary and tips) is $934.40, how much does he earn in tips? 25.____

A. $271.00 B. $274.00 C. $277.00 D. $280.00 E. $283.00

KEY (CORRECT ANSWERS)

1. B
2. E
3. A
4. C
5. C
6. B
7. D
8. E
9. C
10. C
11. E
12. D
13. D
14. C
15. A
16. E
17. B
18. E
19. B
20. A
21. D
22. E
23. C
24. A
25. D

SOLUTIONS TO PROBLEMS

1. CORRECT ANSWER: B
Net pay = \$840 - (.14)(840) - (.035)(840) = \$693.00

2. CORRECT ANSWER: E
Net pay = \$920 - (.14)(920) - (.03)(920) - (.02)(920) = \$745.20

3. CORRECT ANSWER: A
Net pay = \$1030 - (.14)(1030) - 15 - (.02)(1030) = \$850.20

4. CORRECT ANSWER: C
Net pay = \$980 - (.14)(980) - (.03)(980) - (.015)(980) - (.035)(980) = \$764.40

5. CORRECT ANSWER: C
Net pay = \$750 - (.14)(750) - (.03)(750) - (.015)(750) - (.035)(750) = \$585.00

6. CORRECT ANSWER: B
Let x = gross pay. Then, x - .14x - .02x = \$567.00
Simplifying, .84x = 567.00, so x - \$675.00

7. CORRECT ANSWER: D
Let x = gross pay. Then, x - .14x - .03x - .035x = \$890.40. Simplifying, .795x = 890.40, so x = \$1120.00

8. CORRECT ANSWER: E
Let x = gross pay. Then, x - .14x - .015x - .035x = \$607.82. Simplifying, .81x = 607.82, so x = \$750.40

9. CORRECT ANSWER: C
Let x = gross pay. Then, x - .14x - .03x - \$15 - .02x = \$981.46.
Simplifying, .81x = 996.46, so x = \$1230.20. NOTE: Her union dues were \$15, not 1.5% of her gross pay because 1.5% of 1230.20 is \$18.45, which exceeds \$15.

10. CORRECT ANSWER: C
His net pay was affected by a \$15 decrease due to union dues, but also by a (.03)(\$1300) = \$39 increase due to moving out of Detroit. Finally, \$39 - \$15 = \$24

11. CORRECT ANSWER: E
Her net pay was affected by a (.015)(\$880) = \$13.20 increase due to the removal of union dues, and also by a (.03)(\$880) = \$26.40 decrease due to a Detroit city tax. Thus, her net pay was decreased by \$26.40 - \$13.20 = \$13.20.

12. CORRECT ANSWER: D
His medical coverage represents 3.5% of his gross pay. If his gross pay = x, then .035x = \$18.92. Solving, x \$540.60

13. CORRECT ANSWER: D
Net pay = \$430 - (.12)(380) - 3 = \$331.40

14. CORRECT ANSWER: C
Net pay = \$530 - (.12)(400) - (.10)(60) - 3 = \$473.00

15. CORRECT ANSWER: A
Net pay = \$690 - (.12)(400) - (.10)(110) - (.02)(180) = \$627.40

16. CORRECT ANSWER: E
Net pay = \$550 - (.12)(350) - (.02)(200) = \$504.00

17. CORRECT ANSWER: B
Net pay = \$320 - (.12)(320) - 4 = \$277.60

18. CORRECT ANSWER: E
Net pay = \$440 - (.12)(400) - (.10)(40) - 7 = \$381.00

19. CORRECT ANSWER: B
Net pay = \$690 - (.12)(400) - (.10)(160) - 3 - 7 = \$486.00

20. CORRECT ANSWER: A
Net pay = \$440 - (.12)(350) - 3 - 9 = \$386.00

21. CORRECT ANSWER: D
First week net pay = \$710 - (.12)(400) - (.10)(170) - 3 = \$642.00
Second week net pay = \$758.20 - (.12)(400) - (.10) (204.20) - (154)(.02) = \$686.70
Total net pay = \$1328.70

22. CORRECT ANSWER: E
First week net pay = \$710 - (.12)(400) - (.10)(210) - 3 = \$638.00
Second week net pay = \$800 - (.12)(400) - (.10)(400) - 10 = \$702.00
Total net pay = \$1340.00

23. CORRECT ANSWER: C
Let x = gross pay, excluding tips. Then, we have: x + 50 -.12x - 3 - 13 = \$305.04. This simplifes to .88x = 271.04.
Solving, x - \$308.00

24. CORRECT ANSWER: A
Let x = gross pay. Then, x - (.12)(400) - (.10)(x-400) - 5 = \$869.45. Simplifying, x - 48 - .10x + 40 - 5 = 869.45. Then, .90x = 882.45.
Solving, x - \$980.50

25. CORRECT ANSWER: D
Let x = tips earned. Then, \$750 + x - (400)(.12) - (350)(.10) - .02x - 7 = 934.40.
Simplifying, .98x + 660 = 934.40.
Solving, x = \$280.00

TEST 2

DIRECTIONS: Each question or incomplete statement is followed by several suggested answers or completions. Select the one that BEST answers the question or completes the statement. *PRINT THE LETTER OF THE CORRECT ANSWER IN THE SPACE AT THE RIGHT.*

Questions 1-13.

DIRECTIONS: Questions 1 through 13 refer to the following information.

At the Stretch-Tight Rubber Band Company, employees are paid on the 15th day and the last day of every month. Their paychecks are calculated based on the following deductions from their gross pay:

a. Federal tax of 12%
b. State tax of 7%
c. Union dues for union members only. The union dues are calculated as follows: .5% for up to 1 year of employment; 1% for more than 1 year but no more than 5 years of employment; 1.5% for more than 5 years of employment.

1. Jack's gross pay per paycheck is $1000. If he is NOT a union member, what is his net pay? 1.___

   A. $930 B. $880 C. $810 D. $720 E. $640

2. Robin's gross pay per paycheck is $900. If she is a union member with 3 years of employment, what is her net pay? 2.___

   A. $720 B. $729 C. $738 D. $747 E. $756

3. Suzanne's gross pay per paycheck is $1200. If she is a union member with 6 years of employment, what is her net pay? 3.___

   A. $1008 B. $990 C. $972 D. $954 E. $936

4. Mike's gross pay per paycheck is $1600. If he is a union member with 5 months of employment, what is his net pay? 4.___

   A. $1240 B. $1248 C. $1264 D. $1280 E. $1288

5. For the month of May, Bonnie was not a union member up through May 15th, but became a union member on May 16th. She has 8 years of employment, and her gross pay per paycheck is $860. 5.___
   What is her TOTAL net pay for May?

   A. $1347.50 B. $1354.10 C. $1367.40
   D. $1380.30 E. $1393.20

6. For the month of June, Bob was not a union member up through June 15th, but became a union member on June 16th. He has 4 years of employment, and his gross pay per paycheck is $700. 6.___
   What is his TOTAL net pay for June?

   A. $1135 B. $1127 C. $1120 D. $1112 E. $1104

7. Alice is not a union member and her net pay per paycheck is $761.40. What is her gross pay? 7.____

A. $860 B. $900 C. $940 D. $1000 E. $1060

8. Paul is a union member with 3 months of employment. If his net pay per paycheck is $627.90, what is his gross pay? 8.____

A. $760 B. $765 C. $770 D. $775 E. $780

9. Linda is a union member with 7 years of employment. If her net pay per paycheck is $898.35, what is her gross pay? 9.____

A. $1130 B. $1140 C. $1150 D. $1160 E. $1170

10. Ralph is a union member with 2 years of employment. If his net pay per paycheck is $1136, what is his gross pay? 10.____

A. $1438 B. $1420 C. $1410 D. $1402 E. $1388

11. Mary is a union member, and at the end of July of this year, she will have completed 1 year of employment. Her gross pay per paycheck in July is $1050, but beginning in August her gross pay (per paycheck) will become $1180.
What will be the *increase* in her net pay from July to August? 11.____

A. $86.40 B. $98.75 C. $112.45 D. $130.00 E. $143.35

12. Steve is a union member, and at the end of March of this year, he will have completed 5 years of employment. His gross pay per paycheck in March is $980, but beginning in April his gross pay (per paycheck) will become $1100.
What will be the *increase* in his net pay from March to April? 12.____

A. $62.50 B. $73.00 C. $84.50 D. $90.50 E. $96.00

13. Sherry has been a union member up through September of this year. She has 8 months of employment, and her gross pay per paycheck is $800. Beginning in October, she will become a non-union member, and her gross pay (per paycheck) will drop to $660.
What will be the *decrease* in her net pay from September to October? 13.____

A. $109.40 B. $110.80 C. $112.70 D. $113.40 E. $115.60

Questions 14-25.

DIRECTIONS: Questions 14 through 25 refer to the following information.

At the Iron-Clad Steel Company, employees are paid weekly. Their paychecks are calculated based on the following deductions from their gross pay:

a. Federal tax and State tax combined is 16%
b. Union dues for union members only. The union dues are calculated as follows: 2% of an employee's gross pay, up to and including a gross pay of $500, plus of any gross pay in excess of $500.
c. Medical coverage, which is calculated as follows, based on the employee's age: 1.5% of gross pay for employees age 18 through 25; 2.5% of gross pay for employees age 26 through 39; and 5% for employees age 40 or older.

14. Bill's gross pay per paycheck is $820. If he is 24 years old and is not a union member, what is his net pay? 14.____

A. $651.90 B. $664.20 C. $676.50 D. $688.80 E. $701.10

15. Debra's gross pay per paycheck is $740. If she is 41 years old and is not a union member, what is her net pay? 15.____

A. $620.40 B. $602.50 C. $584.60 D. $566.70 E. $548.80

16. Mark's gross pay per paycheck is $700. If he is 32 years old and a union member, what is his net pay? 16.____

A. $564.50 B. $562.50 C. $560.50 D. $558.50 E. $556.50

17. Virginia's gross pay per paycheck is $490. If she is 19 years old and a union member, what is her net pay? 17.____

A. $378.85 B. $382.75 C. $386.65 D. $390.55 E. $394.45

18. Rhonda's gross pay per paycheck is $650. If she is 45 years old and a union member, what is her net pay? 18.____

A. $485.75 B. $502.00 C. $518.25 D. $534.50 E. $550.75

19. For the first week in June, Marianne was not a union member, but became a union member at the beginning of the second week. Her gross pay per paycheck is $880, and she is 38 years old.
What is her TOTAL net pay for these two weeks? 19.____

A. $1448.20 B. $1441.30 C. $1434.40
D. $1427.50 E. $1420.60

20. For the first week in January, Carl was not a union member, but became a union member at the beginning of the second week. His gross pay per paycheck is $470, and he is 22 years old.
What is his TOTAL net pay for these two weeks? 20.____

A. $766.10 B. $775.50 C. $784.90 D. $794.30 E. $803.70

21. Dave's gross pay per paycheck during the first week of October was $450, but his gross pay increased to $550 for the second week in October. If he is 50 years old and a union member, what is his TOTAL net pay for these two weeks? 21.____

A. $805.00 B. $793.50 C. $782.00 D. $770.50 E. $759.00

22. Nancy is not a union member and her net pay per paycheck is $513.45. If she is 35 years old, what is her gross pay? 22.____

A. $615 B. $620 C. $625 D. $630 E. $635

23. Phyllis is not a union member and her net pay per paycheck is $639.90. If she is 43 years old, what is her gross pay? 23.____

A. $780 B. $795 C. $810 D. $825 E. $840

24. Tom is a union member and his net pay per paycheck is $350.90. If he is 21 years old, what is his gross pay? 24.____

A. $436 B. $448 C. $460 D. $472 E. $484

25. Ron is a union member and his net pay per paycheck is $767.80. If he is 37 years old, what is his gross pay? 25.____

A. $972.50 B. $960.00 C. $947.50 D. $935.00 E. $922.50

KEY (CORRECT ANSWERS)

1. C
2. A
3. D
4. E
5. D
6. B
7. C
8. E
9. A
10. B
11. B
12. D
13. A
14. C
15. C
16. D
17. E
18. B
19. E
20. A
21. D
22. D
23. C
24. A
25. B

SOLUTIONS TO PROBLEMS

1. CORRECT ANSWER: C
   Net pay = $1000 - (.12)(1000) - (.07)(1000) = $810

2. CORRECT ANSWER: A
   Net pay = $900 - (.12)(900) - (.07)(900) - (.01)(900) = $720

3. CORRECT ANSWER: D
   Net pay = $1200 - (.12)(1200) - (.07)(1200) - (.015)(1200) = $954

4. CORRECT ANSWER: E
   Net pay = $1600 - (.12)(1600) - (.07)(1600) - (.005)(1600) = $1288

5. CORRECT ANSWER: D
   Net pay = [$860 - (.12)(860) - (.07)(860)] + [$860 - (.12)(860) - (.07)(860) - (.015)(860)] = $1380.30

6. CORRECT ANSWER: B
   Net pay = [$700 - (.12)(700) - (.07)(700)] + [$700 - (.12)(700) - (.07)(700) - (.01)(700)] = $1127

7. CORRECT ANSWER: C
   Let x - gross pay. Then, x - .12x - .07x = 761.40, so .81x = 761.40. Solving, x = $940

8. CORRECT ANSWER: E
   Let x = gross pay. Then, x - .12x - .07x - .005x = 627.90
   So, .805x = 627.90. Solving, x = $780

9. CORRECT ANSWER: A
   Let x = gross pay. Then, x - .12x - .07x - .015x = 898.35,
   So .795x = 898.35.
   Solving, x $1130

10. CORRECT ANSWER: B
    Let x = gross pay. Then, x - .12x - .07x - .01x = 1136
    So, .80x = 1136. Solving, x = $1420

11. CORRECT ANSWER: B
    Mary's net pay in July = $1050 - (.12)(1050) - (.07)(1050) - (.005)(1050) = $845.25. Her net pay in August = $1180 -(.12)(1180) - (.07)(1180) - (.01)(1180) = $944.00
    Then, $944.00 - $845.25 = $98.75

12. CORRECT ANSWER: D
    Steve's net pay in March = $980 - (.12)(980) - (.07)(980)
    - (.01)(980) = 784.00. His net pay in April = $1100 - (.12)(1100)
    - (.07)(1100) - (.015)(1100) = $874.50. Then, $874.50 -$784.00 = $90.50

13. CORRECT ANSWER: A
Sherry's net pay in September = $800 - (.12)(800) - (.07)(800) - (.005)(800) - $644.00. Her net pay in October = $660 -(.12)(660) - (.07)(660) = $534.60. Then, $644.00 - $534.60 = $109.40

14. CORRECT ANSWER: C
Net pay = $820 - (.16)(820) - (.015)(820) = $676.50

15. CORRECT ANSWER: C
Net pay = $740 - (.16)(740) - (.05)(740) = $584.60

16. CORRECT ANSWER: D
Net pay = $700 - (.16)(700) - (.02)(500) - (.01)(200) -(.025)(700) = $558.50

17. CORRECT ANSWER: E
Net pay = $490 - (.16)(490) - (.02)(490) - (.015)(490) = $394.45

18. CORRECT ANSWER: B
Net pay = $650 - (.16)(650) - (.02)(500) - (.01)(150). -(.05)(650) = $502.00

19. CORRECT ANSWER: E
Net pay = [$880 - (.16)(880) - (.025)(880)] + [$880 - (.16)(880) - (.02)(500) - (.01)(380) - (.025)(880)] = $1420.60

20. CORRECT ANSWER: A
Net pay = [$470 - (.16)(470) - (.015)(470)] + [$470 - (.16)(470) - (.02)(470) - (.015)(470)] = $766.10

21. CORRECT ANSWER: D
Net pay = [$450 - (.16)(450) - (.02)(450) - (.05)(450)] + [$550 - (.16)(550) - (.02)(500) - (.01)(50) - (.05)(550)] = $770.50

22. CORRECT ANSWER: D
Let x - gross pay. Then, x - .16x - .025x = 513.45, so, .815x = 513.45. Solving, x = $630

23. CORRECT ANSWER: C
Let x = gross pay. Then, x - .16x - .05x = 639.90, so .79x - 639.90. Solving, x = $810

24. CORRECT ANSWER: A
Let x = gross pay. We can safely assume that his gross pay is less than $500, since all five selections are under $500. Then, x - .16x - .02x - .015x = 350.98, so, .805x = 350.98. Solving, x = $436

25. CORRECT ANSWER: B
Let x = gross pay. Since his gross pay must exceed $500, x - .16x - (.02) (500) - (.01)(x-500) - .025x = 767.80. Simplifying, .805x - 5 - 767.80. Solving, x - $960.00

EXAMINATION SECTION

TEST 1

DIRECTIONS: Each question or incomplete statement is followed by several suggested answers or completions. Select the one that BEST answers the question or completes the statement. *PRINT THE LETTER OF THE CORRECT ANSWER IN THE SPACE AT THE RIGHT.*

Questions 1-5.

DIRECTIONS: Questions 1 through 5 are to be answered on the basis of the extracts from Federal income tax withholding and Social Security tax tables shown below. These tables indicate the amounts which must be withheld from the employee's salary by his employer for Federal income tax and for Social Security. They are based on weekly earnings.

INCOME TAX WITHHOLDING TABLE							
The wages are		And the number of withholding allowances is					
At Least	But Less Than	5	6	7	8	9	10 or More
		The amount of income tax to be withheld shall be					
$300	$320	$24.60	$19.00	$13.80	$ 8.60	$4.00	$ 0
320	340	28.80	22.80	17.40	12.20	7.00	2.80
340	360	33.00	27.00	21.00	15.80	10.60	5.60
360	380	37.20	31.20	25.20	19.40	14.20	9.00
380	400	41.40	34.40	29.40	23.40	17.80	12.60
400	420	45.60	39.60	33.60	27.60	21.40	16.20
420	440	49.80	43.80	37.80	31.80	25.60	19.80
440	460	54.00	48.00	42.00	36.00	29.80	23.80
460	480	58.20	52.20	46.20	40.20	34.00	38.00
480	500	62.40	46.40	40.40	44.40	38.20	32.20

SOCIAL SECURITY TABLE					
WAGES			WAGES		
At Least	But Less Than	Tax to be Withheld	At Least	But Less Than	Tax to be Withheld
$333.18	$333.52	$19.50	$336.60	$336.94	$19.70
333.52	333.86	19.52	336.94	337.28	19.72
333.86	334.20	19.54	337.28	337.62	19.74
334.20	334.54	19.56	337.62	337.96	19.76
334.54	334.88	19.58	337.96	338.30	19.78
334.88	335.22	19.60	338.30	338.64	19.80
335.22	335.56	19.62	338.64	338.98	19.82
335.56	335.90	19.64	338.98	339.32	19.84
335.90	336.24	19.66	339.32	339.66	19.86
336.24	336.60	19.68	339.66	340.00	19.88

1. If an employee has a weekly wage of $379.50 and claims 6 withholding allowances, the amount of income tax to be withheld is 1.____
   A. $27.00 B. $31.20 C. $35.40 D. $37.20

2. An employee had wages of $335.60 for one week. 2.____
   With eight withholding allowances claimed, how much income tax will be withheld from his salary?
   A. $8.60 B. $12.00 C. $13.80 D. $17.40

3. How much social security tax will an employee with weekly wages of $335.60 pay? 3.____
   A. $19.60 B. $19.62 C. $19.64 D. $19.66

4. Mr. Wise earns $339.80 a week and claims seven withholding allowances. 4.____
   What is his take-home pay after income tax and social security tax are deducted?
   A. $300.32 B. $302.52 C. $319.92 D. $322.40

5. If an employee pays $19.74 in social security tax and claims eight withholding allowances, the amount of income tax that should be withheld from his wages is 5.____
   A. $8.60 B. $12.20 C. $13.80 D. $15.80

6. A fundamental rule of bookkeeping states that an individual's assets equal his liabilities plus his proprietorship (ASSETS = LIABILITIES – PROPRIETORSHIP). Which of the following statements logically follows from this rule? 6.____
   A. ASSETS = PROPRIETORSHIP – LIABILITIES
   B. LIABILITIES = ASSETS + PROPRIETORSHIP
   C. PROPRIETORSHIP = ASSETS – LIABILITIES
   D. PROPRIETORSHIP = LIABILITIES + ASSETS

7. Mr. Martin's assets consist of the following: 7.____

Cash on Hand:	$5,233.74
Furniture:	$4,925.00
Government Bonds:	$5,500.00

   What are his TOTAL assets?
   A. $10,158.74 $10,425.00 C. $10,733.74 D. $15,658.74

8. If Mr. Mitchell has $627.04 in his checking account and then writes three checks for $241.74, $13.24, and $101.97, what will be his new balance? 8.____
   A. $257.88 B. $269.08 C. $357.96 D. $368.96

9. An employee's net pay is equal to his total earnings less all deductions. 9.____
   If an employee's total earnings in a pay period are $497.05, what is his NET pay if he has the following deductions: Federal income tax, $90.32; FICA: $28.74; State tax: $18.79; City tax: $7.25; Pension: $1.88?
   A. $351.17 B. $351.07 C. $350.17 D. $350.07

10. A petty cash fund had an opening balance of $85.75 on December 1. Expenditures of $23.00, $15.65, $5.23, $14.75, and $26.38 were made out of his fund during the first 14 days of the month. Then, on December 17, another $38.50 was added to the fund.
If additional expenditures of $17.18, $3.29, and $11.64 were made during the remainder of the month, what was the FINAL balance of the petty cash fund at the end of December? 10.____
A. $6.93 B. $7.13 C. $46.51 D. $91.40

Questions 11-15.

DIRECTIONS: Questions 11 through 15 are to be answered on the basis of the following instructions.

The chart below is used by the loan division of a city retirement system for the following purposes: (1) to calculate the monthly payment a member must pay on an outstanding loan; (2) to calculate how much a member owes on an outstanding loan after he has made a number of payments.

To calculate the amount a member must pay each month in repaying his loan, look at Column II on the chart. You will notice that each entry in Column II corresponds to a number appearing under the *Months* column; for example, 1.004868 corresponds to 1 month, 0.503654 corresponds to 2 months, etc. To calculate the amount a member must pay each month, use the following procedure: multiply the amount of the load by the entry in Column II which corresponds to the number of months over which the load will be paid back. For example, if a loan of $200 is taken out for six months, multiply $200 by 0.169518, the entry in Column II which corresponds to six months.

In order to calculate the balance still owed on an outstanding loan, multiply the monthly payment by the number in Column I which corresponds to the number of monthly payments which remain to be paid on the loan. For example, if a member is supposed to pay $106.00 a month for twelve months, after seven payments, five monthly payments remain. To calculate the balance owed on the loan at this point, multiply the $106.00 monthly payment by 4.927807, the number in Column I that corresponds to five months.

Months	Column I	Column II
1	0.995156	1.004868
2	1.985491	0.503654
3	2.971029	0.336584
4	3.951793	0.253050
5	4.927807	0.202930
6	5.899092	0.169518
7	6.865673	0.145652
8	7.827572	0.127754
9	8.784811	0.113833
10	9.737414	0.102697
11	10.685402	0.093586
12	11.628798	0.085994
13	12.567624	0.079570
14	13.501902	0.074064
15	14.431655	0.069292

11. If Mr. Carson borrows $1,500 for eight months, how much will he have to pay back each month? 11.____
    A. $187.16 B. $191.63 C. $208.72 D. $218.65

12. If a member borrows $2,400 for one year, the amount he will have to pay back each month is 12.____
    A. $118.78 B. $196.18 C. $202.28 D. $206.38

13. Mr. Elliott borrowed $1,700 for a period of fifteen months. Each month he will have to pay back 13.____
    A. $117.80 B. $116.96 C. $107.79 D. $101.79

14. Mr. Aylward is paying back a thirteen-month loan at the rate of $173.13 a month. If he has already made six monthly payments, how much does he owe on the outstanding loan? 14.____
    A. $1,027.38 B. $1,178.75 C. $1,188.65 D. $1,898.85

15. A loan was taken out for 15 months, and the monthly payment was $104.75. After two monthly payments, how much was still owed on this load? 15.____
    A. $515.79 B. $863.89 C. $1,116.76 D. $1,316.46

16. The ABC Corporation had a gross income of $125,500.00 in 2015. Of this, it paid 60% for overhead. If the gross income for 2016 increased by $6,500 and the cost of overhead increased to 61% of gross income, how much more did it pay for overhead in 2016 than in 2015? 16.____
    A. $1,320 B. $5,220 C. $7,530 D. $8,052

17. After one year, Mr. Richards paid back a total of $1,695.00 as payment for a $1,500.00 loan. All the money paid over $1,500.00 was simple interest. The interest charge was MOST NEARLY 17.____
A. 13% B. 11% C. 9% D. 7%

18. A checking account has a balance of $253.36. 18.____
If deposits of $36.95, $210.23, and $7.34 and withdrawals of $117.35, $23.37, and $15.98 are made, what is the NEW balance of the account?
A. $155.54 B. $351.18 C. $364.58 D. $664.58

19. In 2015, the W Realty Company spent 27% of its income on rent. 19.____
If it earned $97,254.00 in 2015, the amount it paid for rent was
A. $26.258.58 B. $26,348.58 C. $27,248.58 D. $27,358.58

20. Six percent simple annual interest on $2,436.18 is MOST NEARLY 20.____
A. $145.08 B. $145.17 c. $146.08 D. $146.17

21. Assume that the XYZ Company has $10,402.72 cash on hand. 21.____
If it pays $699.83 of this for rent, the amount of cash on hand would be
A. $9,792.89 B. $9,702.89 C. $9,692.89 D. $9,602.89

22. On January 31, Mr. Warren's checking account had a balance of $933.68. 22.____
If he deposited $36.40 on February 2, $126.00 on February 9, and $90.02 on February 16 and wrote no checks during this period, what was the balance of his account on February 17?
A. $680.26 B. $681.26 C. $1,186.10 D. $1,187.00

23. Multiplying a number by .75 is the same as 23.____
A. multiplying it by 2/3
B. dividing it by 2/3
C. multiplying it by 3/4
D. dividing it by 3/4

24. In City Agency A, 2/3 of the employees are enrolled in a retirement system. 24.____
City Agency B has the same number of employees as Agency A, and 60% of these are enrolled in a retirement system.
If Agency A has a total of 660 employees, how many MORE employees does it have enrolled in a retirement system than does Agency B?
B. 36 B. 44 C. 56 D. 66

25. Net Worth is equal to Assets minus Liabilities. 25.____
If, at the end of year, a textile company had assets of $98,695.83 and liabilities of $59,238.29, what was its net worth?
A. $38,478.54 B. $38,488.64 C. $39,457.54 D. $48,557.54

KEY (CORRECT ANSWERS)

1. B
2. B
3. C
4. B
5. B

6. C
7. D
8. B
9. D
10. B

11. B
12. D
13. A
14. C
15. D

16. B
17. A
18. B
19. A
20. D

21. B
22. C
23. C
24. B
25. C

TEST 2

DIRECTIONS: Each question or incomplete statement is followed by several suggested answers or completions. Select the one that BEST answers the question or completes the statement. *PRINT THE LETTER OF THE CORRECT ANSWER IN THE SPACE AT THE RIGHT.*

Questions 1-10.

DIRECTIONS: Questions 1 through 10 below present the identification numbers, initials, and last names of employees enrolled in a city retirement system. You are to choose the option (A, B, C, or D) that has the IDENTICAL identification number, initials, and last name as those given in each question.

<u>Sample Question</u>
B145698 JL Jones

A. B146798 JL Jones　　B. B145698 JL Jonas
C. P145698 JL Jones　　D. B145698 JL Jones

The correct answer is D. Only Option D shows the identification number, initials, and last name exactly as they are in the sample question. Options A, B, and C have errors in the identification number or last name.

1. J297483 PL Robinson　　1.____
 A. J294783 PL Robinson　　B. J297483 PL Robinson
 C. J297483 Pl Robinson　　D. J297843 PL Robinson

2. S497662 JG Schwartz　　2.____
 B. S497662 JG Schwarz　　B. S497762 JG Schwartz
 C. S497662 JG Schwartz　　D. S497663 JG Schwartz

3. G696436 LN Alberton　　3.____
 A. G696436 LM Alberton　　B. G696436 LN Albertson
 C. G696346 LN Albertson　　D. G696436 LN Alberton

4. R774923 AD Aldrich　　4.____
 A. R774923 AD Aldrich　　B. R744923 AD Aldrich
 C. R774932 AP Aldrich　　D. R774932 AD Allrich

5. N239638 RP Hrynyk　　5.____
 A. N236938 PR Hrynyk　　B. N236938 RP Hrynyk
 C. N239638 PR Hrynyk　　D. N239638 Hrynyk

6. R156949 LT Carlson　　6.____
 A. R156949 LT Carlton　　B. R156494 LT Carlson
 C. R159649 LT Carlton　　D. R156949 LT Carlson

7. T524697 MN Orenstein　　7.____
 A. T524697 MN Orenstein　　B. T524967 MN Orinstein
 C. T524697 NM Ornstein　　D. T524967 NM Orenstein

8. L346239 JD Remsen 8.____
   A. L346239 JD Remson
   B. L364239 JD Remsen
   C. L346329 JD Remsen
   D. L346239 JD Remsen

9. P966438 SB Rieperson 9.____
   A. P996438 SB Rieperson
   B. P466438 SB Reiperson
   C. R996438 SB Rieperson
   D. P966438 SB Rieperson

10. D749382 CD Thompson 10.____
   A. P749382 CD Thompson
   B. D749832 CD Thomsonn
   C. D749382 CD Thompson
   D. D749823 CD Thomspon

Questions 11-20.

DIRECTIONS: Assume that each of the capital letters in the table below represents the name of an employee enrolled in the city's employees' personnel system. The number directly beneath the letter represents the agency for which the employee works, and the small letter directly beneath represents the code for the employee's account.

Name of Employee	L	O	T	Q	A	M	R	N	C
Agency	3	4	5	9	8	7	2	1	6
Account Code	r	f	b	i	d	t	g	e	n

In each of the following Questions 11 through 20, the agency code numbers and the account code letters in Columns 2 and 3 should correspond to the capital letters in Column 1 and should be in the same consecutive order. For each question, look at each column carefully and mark your answer as follows:

If there are one or more errors in Column 2 only, mark your answer A.
If there are one or more errors in Column 3 only, mark your answer B.
I there are one or more errors in Column 2 and one or more errors in Column 3, mark your answer C.
If there are NO errors in either column, mark your answer D.

Sample Question

Column 1	Column 2	Column 3
TQLMOC	583746	birtfn

In Column 2, the second agency code number (corresponding to letter Q) should be 9, not 8. Column 3 is coded correctly to Column 1. Since there is an error only in Column 2, the correct answer is A.

	COLUMN 1	COLUMN 2	COLUMN 3	
11.	QLNRCA	931268	iregnd	11.____
12.	NRMOTC	127546	egftbn	12.____
13.	RCTALM	265837	gndbrt	13.____
14.	TAMLON	578341	bdtrfe	14.____
15.	ANTORM	815427	debigt	15.____
16.	MRALON	728341	tgdrfe	16.____
17.	CTNQRO	657924	ndeigf	17.____
18.	QMROTA	972458	itgfbd	18.____
19.	RQMCOL	297463	gitnfr	19.____
20.	NOMRTQ	147259	eftgbi	20.____

Questions 21-25.

DIRECTIONS: Questions 21 through 25 are to be answered SOLELY on the basis of the following passage.

The city may issue its own bonds or it may purchase bonds as an investment. Bonds may be issued in various denominations, and the face value of the bond is its par value. Before purchasing a bond, the investor desires to know the rate of income that the investment may yield in computing the yield on a bond, it is assumed that the investor will keep the bond until the date of maturity, except for callable bonds which are not considered in this passage. To compute exact yield is a complicated mathematical problem, and scientifically prepared tables are generally used to avoid such computation. However, the approximate yield can be computed much more easily. In computing approximate yield, the accrued interest on the date of purchase should be ignored because the buyer who pays accrued interest to the seller receives it again at the next interest date. Bonds bought at a premium (which cost more) yield a lower rate of income than the same bonds bought at par (face value), and bounds bought at a discount (which cost less) yield a higher rate of income than the same bonds bought at par.

21. An investor bought a $10,000 city bond paying 6% interest. 21.____
Which of the following purchase prices would indicate that the bond was bought at a premium?
A. $9,000 B. $9,400 C. $10,000 D. $10,600

22. During 2016, a particular $10,000 bond paying 7 ½% sold at fluctuating prices. 22.____
Which of the following prices would indicate that the bond was bought at a discount?
A. $9,800 B. $10,000 C. $10,200 D. $10,750

23. A certain group of bonds was sold in denominations of$5,000, $10,000, $20,000, and $50,000. 23.____
In the following list of four purchase prices, which one is MOST likely to represent a bond sold at par value?
A. $10,500 B. $20,000 C. $22,000 D. $49,000

24. When computing the approximate yield on a bond, it is DESIRABLE to 24.____
A. assume the bond was purchased at par
B. consult scientifically prepared tables
C. ignore accrued interest on the date of purchase
D. wait until the bond reaches maturity

25. Which of the following is MOST likely to be an exception to the information provided in the above passage? 25.____
Bonds
A. purchased at a premium
B. sold at par
C. sold before maturity
D. which are callable

KEY (CORRECT ANSWERS)

1. B
2. C
3. D
4. A
5. D

6. D
7. A
8. D
9. D
10. C

11. D
12. C
13. B
14. A
15. B

16. D
17. C
18. D
19. A
20. D

21. D
22. A
23. B
24. C
25. D

TEST 3

DIRECTIONS: Each question or incomplete statement is followed by several suggested answers or completions. Select the one that BEST answers the question or completes the statement. *PRINT THE LETTER OF THE CORRECT ANSWER IN THE SPACE AT THE RIGHT.*

Questions 1-6.

DIRECTIONS: Questions 1 through 6 consist of computations of addition, subtraction, multiplication, and division. For each question, do the computation indicated, and choose the correct answer from the four choices given.

1. ADD:
8936
7821
8953
4297
9785
6579 1.____

A. 45371 B. 45381 C. 46371 D. 46381

2. SUBTRACT:
95,432
67,596 2.____

A. 27,836 B. 27,846 C. 27,936 D. 27,946

3. MULTIPLY:
987
867 3.____

A. 854609 B. 854729 C. 855709 D. 855729

4. DIVIDE: 59)321439.0 4.____

A. 5438.1 B. 5447.1 C. 5448.1 D. 5457.1

5. DIVIDE: .057)721 5.____

A. 12,648.0 B. 12,648.1 C. 12,649.0 D. 12,649.1

6. ADD: 1/2 + 5/7 6.____

A. 1 3/14 B. 1 2/7 C. 1 5/14 D. 1 3/7

7. If the total number of employees in one city agency increased from 1,927 to 2,006 during a certain year, the percentage increase in the number of employees for that year is MOST NEARLY 7.____

A. 4% B. 5% C. 6% D. 7%

8. During a single fiscal year, which totaled 248 workdays, one account clerk verified 1,488 purchase vouchers. 8.____
Assuming a normal work week of five days, what is the average number of vouchers verified by the account clerk in a one-week period during this fiscal year?
A. 25 B. 30 C. 35 D. 40

9. If the city department of purchase bought 190 computers for $793.50 each and 208 computers for $839.90 each, the TOTAL price paid for these computers is 9.____
A. $315,813.00 B. $325,464.20
C. $334,279.20 D. $335,863.00

Questions 10-14.

DIRECTIONS: Questions 10 through 14 are to be answered SOLELY on the basis of the information given in the following paragraph.

Since discounts are in common use in the commercial world and apply to purchases made by government agencies as well as business firms, it is essential that individuals in both public and private employment who prepare bills, check invoices, prepare payment vouchers, or write checks to pay bills have an understanding of the terms used. These include cash or time discount, trade discount, and disconnect series. A cash or time discount offers a reduction in price to the buyer for the prompt payment of the bill and is usually expressed as a percentage with a time requirement, stated in days, within which the bill must be paid in order to earn the discount. An example would be 3/10, meaning a 3% discount may be applied to the bill if the payment is forwarded to the vendor within ten days. On an invoice, the cash discount terms are usually followed by the net terms, which is the time in days allowed for ordinary payment of the bill. Thus, 3/10, Net 30 means that full payment is expected in thirty days if the cash discount of 3% is not taken for having paid the bill within ten days. When the expression Terms Net Cash is listed on a bill, it means that no deduction for early payment is allowed. A trade discount is normally applied to list prices by a manufacturer to show the actual price to retailers so that they may know their cost and determine markups that will allow them to operate competitively and at a profit. A trade discount is applied by the seller to the list price and is independent of a cash or time discount. Discounts may also be used by manufacturers to adjust prices charged to retailers without changing list prices. This is usually done by series discounting and is expressed as a series of percentages. To compute a series discount, such as 40%, 20%, 10%, first apply the 40% discount to the list price, then apply the 20% discount to the remainder, and finally apply the 10% discount to the second remainder.

10. According to the above passage, trade discounts are 10.____
A. applied by the buyer B. independent of cash discounts
C. restricted to cash sales D. used to secure rapid payment of bills

11. According to the above passage, if the sales terms 5/10, Net 60 appear on a bill in the amount of $100 dated December 5, 2016 and the buyer submits his payment on December 15, 2016, his PROPER payment should be 11.____
A. $60 B. $90 C. $95 D. $100

12. According to the above passage, if a manufacturer gives a trade discount of 40% for an item with a list price of $250 and the terms are Net Cash, the price a retail merchant is required to pay for this item is 12.____
    A. $250 B. $210 C. $150 D. $100

13. According to the above passage, a series discount of 25%, 20%, 10% applied to a list price of $200 results in an ACTUAL price to the buyer of 13.____
    A. $88 B. $90 C. $108 D. $110

14. According to the above passage, if a manufacturer gives a trade discount of 50% and the terms are 6/10, Net 30, the cost to a retail merchant of an item with a list price of $500 and for which he takes the time discount is 14.____
    A. $220 B. $235 C. $240 D. $250

Questions 15-22.

DIRECTIONS: Questions 15 through 22 each show in Column I the information written on five cards (lettered j, k, l, m, n) which have to be filed. You are to choose the option (lettered A, B, C, or D) in Column II which BEST represents the proper order of filing according to the information, rules, and sample question given below.

A file card record is kept of the work assignments for all the employees in a certain bureau. On each card is the employee's name, the date of work assignment, and the work assignment code number. The cards are to be filed according to the following rules:

FIRST: File in alphabetical order according to employee's name.

SECOND: When two or more cards have the same employee's name, file according to the assignment date, beginning with the earliest date.

THIRD: When two or more cards have the same employee's name and the same date, file according to the work assignment number beginning with the lowest number.

Column II shows the cards arranged in four different orders. Pick the option (A, B, C, or D) in Column II which shows the correct arrangement of the cards according to th above filing rules.

SAMPLE QUESTION

Column I	Column II
j. Cluney 4/8/02 (486503)	A. k, l, m, j, n
k. Roster 5/10/01 (246611)	B. k, n, j, l, m
l. Altool 10/15/02 (711433)	C. l, k, j, m, n
m. Cluney 12/18/02 (527610)	D. l, n, j, m, k
n. Cluney 4/8/02 (486500)	

The correct way to file the cards is:

l. Altool 10/15/02 (71143)
n. Cluney 4/8/02 (486500)
j. Cluney 4/8/02 (486503)
m. Cluney 12/18/02 (527610)
k. Roster 5/10/01 (246611)

The correct filing order is shown by the letters l, n, j, m, k. The answer to the sample question is the letter D, which appears in front of the letters l, n, j, m, k in Column II.

	COLUMN I	COLUMN II	
15.	j. Smith 3/19/03 (662118) k. Turner 4/16/99 (481349) l. Terman 3/20/02 (210229) m. Smyth 3/20/02 (481359) n. Terry 5/11/01 (672128)	A. j, m, l, n, k B. j, l, n, m, k C. k, n, m, l, j D. j, n, k, l, m	15.____
16.	j. Ross 5/29/02 (396118) k. Rosner 5/29/02 (439281) l. Rose 7/19/02 (723456) m. Rosen 5/29/03 (829692) n. Ross 5/29/02 (399118)	A. l, m, k, n, j B. m, l, k, n, j C. l, m, k, j, n D. m, l, j, n, k	16.____
17.	j. Sherd 10/12/99 (552368) k. Snyder 11/12/99 (539286) l. Shindler 10/13/98 (426798) m. Scherld 10/12/99 (552386) n. Schneider 11/12/99 (798213)	A. n, m, k, j, l B. j, m, l, k, n C. m, k, n, j. l D. m, n, j, l, k	17.____
18.	j. Carter 1/16/02 (489636) k. Carson 2/16/01 (392671) l. Carter 1/16/01 (486936) m. Carton 3/15/00 (489639) n. Carson 2/16/01 (392617)	A. k, n, j, l, m B. n, k, m, l, j C. n, k, l, j, m D. k, n, l, j, m	18.____
19.	j. Thomas 3/18/99 (763182) k. Tompkins 3/19/00 (928439) l. Thomson 3/21/00 (763812) m. Thompson 3/18/99 (924893) n. Tompson 3/19/99 (928793)	A. m, l, j, k, n B. j, m, l, k, n C. j, l, n, m, k D. l, m, j, n, k	19.____
20.	j. Breit 8/10/03 (345612) k. Briet 5/21/00 (837543) l. Bright 9/18/99 (931827) m. Breit 3/7/98 (553984) n. Brent 6/14/04 (682731)	A. m, j, n, k, l B. n, m, j, k, l C. m, j, k, l, n D. j, m, k, l, n	20.____

COLUMN I	COLUMN II	
21. j. Roberts 10/19/02 (581932)	A. n, k, l, m, j	21.____
k. Rogers 8/9/00 (638763)	B. n, k, l, j, m	
l. Rogerts 7/15/97 (105689)	C. k, n, l, m, j	
m. Robin 3/8/92 (287915)	D. j, m, k, n, l	
n. Rogers 4/2/04 (736921)		
22. j. Hebert 4/28/02 (719468)	A. n, k, j, m, l	22.____
k. Herbert 5/8/01 (938432)	B. j, l, n, k, m	
l. Helbert 9/23/04 (832912)	C. l, j, k, n, m	
m. Herbst 7/10/03 (648599)	D. l, j, n, k, m	
n. Herbert 5/8/01 (487627)		

23. In order to pay its employees, the Convex Company obtained bills and coins in the following denominations: 23.____

Denomination	$20	$10	$5	$1	$.50	$.25	$.10	$.05	$.01
Number	317	122	38	73	69	47	39	25	36

What was the TOTAL amount of cash obtained?
A. $7,874.76 B. $7,878.00 C. $7,889.25 D. $7,924.35

24. H. Partridge receives a weekly gross salary (before deductions) of $596.25. Through weekly payroll deductions of $19.77, he is paying back a load he took from his pension fund. 24.____
If other fixed weekly deductions amount to $184.14, how much pay would Mr. Partridge take home over a period of 33 weeks?
A. $11,446.92 B. $12,375.69 C. $12,947.22 D. $19,676.25

25. Mr. Robertson is a city employee enrolled in a city retirement system. He has taken out a loan from the retirement fund and is paying it back at the rate of $14.90 every two weeks. 25.____
In eighteen weeks, how much money will he have paid back on the loan?
A. $268.20 B. $152.80 C. $124.10 D. $67.05

26. In 2015, the Iridor Book Company had the following expenses: rent, $6,500; overhead, $52,585; inventory, $35,700; and miscellaneous, $1,275. 26.____
If all of these expenses went up 18% in 2016, what would they TOTAL in 2016?
A. $17,290.80 B. $78,768.20 C. $96,060.00 D. $113,350.80

27. Ms. Ranier had a gross salary of $355.36, paid once every week. 27.____
If the deductions from each paycheck are $62.72, $25.13, $6.29, and $1,27, how much money would Ms. Ranier take home in four weeks?
A. $1,039.80 B. $1,421.44 C. $2,079.60 D. $2,842.88

28. Mr. Martin had a net income of $19,100 for the year. 28.____
If he spent 34% on rent and household expenses, 3% on house furnishings, 25% on clothes, and 36% on food, how much was left for savings and other expenses?
A. $196.00 B. $382.00 C. $649.40 D. $1,960.00

29. Mr. Elsberg can pay back a loan of $1,800 from the city employees' retirement system if he pays back $36.69 every two weeks for two full years. 29.____
At the end of the two years, how much more than the original $1,800 he borrowed will Mr. Elsberg have paid back?
A. $53.94 B. $107.88 C. $190.79 D. $214.76

30. Mrs. Nusbaum is a city employee, receiving a gross salary (salary before deductions) of $31,200. Every two weeks, the following deductions are taken out of her salary: Federal Income Tax, $243.96; FICA, $66.39; State Tax, $44.58; City Tax, $20.91; Health Insurance, $4.71. 30.____
If Mrs. Nusbaum's salary and deductions remained the same for a full calendar year, what would her NET salary (gross salary less deductions) be in that year?
A. $9,894.30 B. $21,305.70 C. $28,118.25 D. $30,819.45

KEY (CORRECT ANSWERS)

1.	C	11.	C	21.	D
2.	A	12.	C	22.	B
3.	D	13.	C	33.	A
4.	C	14.	B	24.	C
5.	D	15.	A	25.	C
6.	A	16.	C	26.	D
7.	A	17.	D	27.	A
8.	B	18.	C	28.	B
9.	B	19.	B	29.	B
10.	B	20.	A	30.	B

EXAMINATION SECTION
TEST 1

DIRECTIONS: Each question or incomplete statement is followed by several suggested answers or completions. Select the one that BEST answers the question or completes the statement. *PRINT THE LETTER OF THE CORRECT ANSWER IN THE SPACE AT THE RIGHT.*

Questions 1-7.

DIRECTIONS: Questions 1 through 7 are to be answered on the basis of the following income statement.

Laura Lee's Bridal Shop
Income Statement
For the Year Ended December 31, 2018

Revenue:		
New & Used Bridal Gowns & Accessories		$55,000
Expenses:		
Advertisement Expense	$ 2,000	
Salaries Expense	12,000	
Dry cleaning & Alterations	10,000	
Utilities	1,500	
Total Expenses		25,500
Net Income		$29,500

1. What is the period of time covered by this income statement? 1.____

   A. January-December 2017
   B. December 2018
   C. January 2017-December 2018
   D. January-December 2018

2. What is the source of the revenue? 2.____

   A. New and used bridal gowns, advertisements, salaries, dry cleaning, and utilities
   B. Advertisements, salaries, dry cleaning, alterations, and utilities
   C. New and used bridal gowns and accessories
   D. Net income

3. What is the total revenue? 3.____

   A. $25,500 B. $55,000 C. $29,500 D. $79,500

4. Which of the following are expenses? 4.____

   A. Salaries
   B. New and used bridal gowns and accessories
   C. Revenue
   D. New and used bridal gowns, advertisements, and dry cleaning

5. What are the total expenses? 5.____

   A. $55,000 B. $29,500 C. $79,500 D. $25,500

6. There is a resulting net income because 6.____

   A. total revenue and total expenses are combined
   B. net income is greater than total revenue
   C. the total revenue is greater than total expenses
   D. the total revenue is less than total expenses

7. Is this statement an interim statement? 7.____

   A. *Yes*, because it covers an entire accounting period
   B. *No*, because it covers an entire accounting period
   C. *Yes*, because it covers a period of less than a year
   D. *No*, because it covers a period of more than a year

8. What is the name of the accounting report that may show either a net profit or a net loss for an accounting period? 8.____

   A. Income statement
   B. Balance sheet
   C. Statement of capital
   D. Classified balance sheet

9. What are the two main parts of the body of the income statement? 9.____

   A. Cash and Capital
   B. Revenue and Expenses
   C. Liabilities and Capital
   D. Assets and Notes Payable

10. If total revenue exceeds total expenses for an accounting period, what is the difference called? 10.____

    A. Gross income
    B. Total liabilities
    C. Total assets
    D. Net income

11. In the body of a balance sheet, what are the three sections called? 11.____

    A. Assets and liabilities
    B. Cash, liabilities, and revenue
    C. Assets, liabilities, and capital
    D. Revenue, assets, and capital

12. What business record shows the results of the proprietor's borrowing assets from the business, usually in anticipation of profits? 12.____

    A. Proprietor's withdrawals
    B. Accounts payable
    C. Liabilities and Capital
    D. Total liabilities

Questions 13-24.

DIRECTIONS: For each transaction given for Mona's Magic Moments Hair Salon in Questions 13 through 24, identify which journal the transaction should be recorded in.

13. April 1: Mona, the owner, paid the month's rent - $600.00; check no. 356. 13.____

    A. General
    B. Cash disbursements
    C. Purchases
    D. Sales

14. April 6: the salon purchased $300.00 worth of styling products on account from Pomme de Terre Company. 14.____

A. Cash disbursements
B. General
C. Sales
D. Purchases

15. April 8: sold $100.00 worth of hair products on account to Mrs. Angela Bray. 15.____

A. Sales
B. Purchases
C. Cash disbursements
D. General

16. April 11: the owner, Mona Ramen, withdrew $80.00 of styling products for personal use. 16.____

A. Sales
B. Cash receipts
C. General
D. Cash disbursements

17. April 13: paid Pomme de Terre Company $300.00 on account; check 357. 17.____

A. Purchases
B. Cash disbursements
C. Cash receipts
D. General

18. April 15: cash sales to date were $4,607.00. 18.____

A. Cash disbursements
B. Purchases
C. Sales
D. General

19. April 17: issued credit slip #17 to Mrs. Angela Bray for $25.00 for merchandise returned. 19.____

A. Cash disbursements
B. Cash receipts
C. Sales
D. General

20. April 19: paid electric bill for $250.00; check no. 358. 20.____

A. Cash disbursements
B. Purchases
C. General
D. Cash receipts

21. April 21: received $75.00 from Mrs. Angela Bray for balance due on account. 21.____

A. Sales
B. Cash disbursements
C. Cash receipts
D. Purchases

22. April 23: sold $88.00 of hair products on account to Ms. Tania Alioto. 22.____

A. Purchases
B. Sales
C. Cash disbursements
D. Cash receipts

23. April 27: purchased $500.00 of equipment from Salon Stylings Merchandisers on account. 23.____

A. Cash disbursements
B. Sales
C. General
D. Purchases

24. April 30: cash sales to date were $5023.00. 24.____

A. Purchases
B. Sales
C. Cash receipts
D. General

Questions 25-30.

DIRECTIONS: Questions 25 through 30 are to be answered on the basis of the following ledger for a barbecue take-out restaurant owned and operated by Ruby Joiner.

Cash

Debit	Credit
450	150
212	125
328	440
172	125
250	70
275	150
325	50

Accounts Receivable

Debit	Credit
360	170
250	100
165	120
100	60

Delivery Equipment

Debit	Credit
5,000	
4,000	
3,000	

Supplies

Debit	Credit
40	
65	
30	
25	

Ruby Joiner, Capital

Debit	Credit
	8,200
	2,000
	2,097

Accounts Payable

Debit	Credit
10	600
15	300
	200

Ruby Joiner, Drawing

Debit	Credit
225	
175	
200	

Advertising Expense

Debit	Credit
40	
45	

Delivery Income

Debit	Credit
	400
	350
	250
	100

Trucking Expense

Debit	Credit
100	
50	

Telephone Expense

Debit	Credit
80	
40	
20	

25. What is the balance on the Cash account shown above? 25.____

A. 2,012.00 B. 1,110.00 C. 3,122.00 D. 902.00

26. What is the balance on the Accounts receivable account shown above? 26.____

A. 425.00 B. 875.00 C. 450.00 D. 1315.00

27. What is the balance on the Accounts payable account shown above? 27.____

A. 1100.00 B. 1075.00 C. 25.00 D. 1125.00

28. Which of the above accounts has a balance of 1100.00? 28.____

A. Accounts payable B. Delivery Income
C. Cash D. Delivery equipment

29. Which of the above accounts has a balance of 12,000.00? 29.____

A. Ruby Joiner, Capital
B. Cash and Accounts receivable combined
C. Delivery equipment
D. None of the accounts

30. If you made a balance sheet out of the information listed above, Ruby Joiner's total assets would be 30.____

A. 14,472.00 B. 12,297.00 C. 13,392.00 D. 13,487.00

Questions 31-34.

DIRECTIONS: Questions 31 through 34 are to be answered on the basis of the following information, to be included on a checking deposit ticket.

Five $20 bills; 11 $10 bills; 6 $5 bills; 47 $1 bills; 200 half dollars; 120 quarters; 112 dimes; 320 nickels; 67 pennies. Second National Bank (73-124) check of 152.34; Bank of the Midwest (13-298) check of 68.37; Great National Bank (32-165) check of 185.06.

31. What is the TOTAL currency for this deposit? 31.____

A. $387 B. $287 C. $444.87 D. $157.87

32. What is the TOTAL coin for this deposit? 32.____

A. $387 B. $287 C. $444.87 D. $157.87

33. What is the check total for this deposit? 33.____

A. $692.77 B. $406 C. $405.77 D. $850.64

34. What is the TOTAL deposit? 34.____

A. $444.87 B. $692.77 C. $851 D. $850.64

Questions 35-37.

DIRECTIONS: Questions 35 through 37 are to be answered on the basis of the following petty cash journal.

Date	Receipt No.	To Whom Paid	For What	Acct.#	Amount
10/2	1	Anna Jones - Mail	Postage	548	13.50
10/2	2	Jim Collins	Messenger	525	5.75
10/4	3	Anna Jones - Mail	Postage	548	13.50
10/5	4	Lucky Stores	Coffee	515	7.34
10/6	5	Tom Allen	Lunch w/customer	525	11.38

35. What is the TOTAL disbursement from this fund for the time period 10/1 through 10/6? 35.____

A. $51.47 B. $40.09 C. $61.47 D. $26.59

36. How much money was disbursed to Account #548 during the time period 10/1-10/16? 36.____

A. $51.47 B. $26 C. $27 D. $34.34

37. If the fund began the month with a total of $100.00, what amount was left in the fund at the end of business on 10/5? 37.____

A. $48.53 B. $59.91 C. $51.47 D. $40.09

Questions 38-40.

DIRECTIONS: Questions 38 through 40 are to be answered on the basis of the following information.

A promissory note dated December 1, 2018, bearing interest at a rate of 12% and due in 90 days, is sent to a creditor. The face value of the note is $900.

38. What is the due date of the promissory note? 38.____

A. January 15, 2019
B. March 1, 2019
C. February 1, 2019
D. December 31, 2018

39. What is the TOTAL interest that will be earned on the note? 39.____

A. $27
B. $270
C. $108
D. $10.80

40. What interest will be earned on the note for the old accounting period (December 1-31)? 40.____

A. $90
B. $36
C. $9
D. $3.60

KEY (CORRECT ANSWERS)

1. D	11. C	21. C	31. B
2. C	12. A	22. B	32. D
3. B	13. B	23. D	33. C
4. A	14. D	24. B	34. D
5. D	15. A	25. D	35. A
6. C	16. C	26. A	36. C
7. B	17. B	27. B	37. B
8. A	18. C	28. B	38. B
9. B	19. D	29. C	39. A
10. D	20. A	30. D	40. C

TEST 2

DIRECTIONS: Each question or incomplete statement is followed by several suggested answers or completions. Select the one that BEST answers the question or completes the statement. *PRINT THE LETTER OF THE CORRECT ANSWER IN THE SPACE AT THE RIGHT.*

Questions 1-4.

DIRECTIONS: Questions 1 through 4 are to be answered on the basis of the following information, to be included in a deposit slip.

14 twenty dollar bills	63 quarters
52 ten dollar bills	22 dimes
12 five dollar bills	44 nickels
43 one dollar bills	70 pennies

Checks: $236.34 and $129.72

1. What is the TOTAL amount of currency for this deposit? 1.____

   A. $923.85 B. $1269.06 C. $903.00 D. $1299.91

2. What is the TOTAL amount of coin for this deposit? 2.____

   A. $20.85 B. $923.85 C. $903.00 D. $1299.91

3. What is the TOTAL amount of check for this deposit? 3.____

   A. $20.85 B. $366.06 C. $1299.91 D. $903.00

4. What is the TOTAL deposit for this slip? 4.____

   A. $1269.06 B. $903.00 C. $923.85 D. $1289.91

Questions 5-7.

DIRECTIONS: Questions 5 through 7 are to be answered on the basis of the following information.

Angela Martinez's last check stub balance was $675.50. Her bank statement balance dated April 30 was $652.00. A $250 deposit was in transit on that date. Outstanding checks were as follows: No. 127, $65.00; No. 129, $203.50; No. 130, $50.00. The bank service charge for the month was $5.00.

5. What was Angela Martinez's available checkbook balance on April 30? 5.____

   A. $652.00 B. $338.50 C. $583.50 D. $675.50

6. In order to reconcile her checkbook balance with her bank statement balance, what must Angela Martinez do? 6.____

   A. Add her checkbook balance to the balance on her bank statement
   B. Subtract her checkbook balance from the balance on her bank statement

C. Ignore her checkbook balance and adopt the balance on her bank statement
D. Adjust the checkbook balance by adding deposits and debiting outstanding checks and charges

7. The check stub balance referred to in the problem refers to the 7.____

A. last check Angela Martinez recorded in her checkbook
B. amount of money left in Angela Martinez's account according to her own calculations based on the checks, charges, and deposits she has written and recorded
C. amount of money left in Angela Martinez's account according to the bank's calculations based on the checks, charges, and deposits posted to her account
D. number of checks left in her checkbook

Questions 8-9.

DIRECTIONS: Questions 8 and 9 are to be answered on the basis of the following information.

Tu Nguyen, an interior designer, received his June bank statement on July 2. The balance was $622.66. His last check stub balance was $700. On comparing the two, he noticed that a deposit of $275 made on June 30 was not included on the statement; also, a bank service charge of $4 was deducted. Outstanding checks were as follows: No. 331, $97.50; No. 332, $207; No. 335, $25.40; and No. 336, $68.97.

8. What is Nguyen's CORRECT available bank balance? 8.____

A. $494.79 B. $897.66 C. $700.00 D. $219.79

9. The bank statement balance referred to in the problem refers to the 9.____

A. last check Tu Nguyen recorded in his checkbook
B. last check presented for payment to Tu Nguyen's account
C. amount of money left in Tu Nguyen's account according to the bank's calculations based on the checks, charges, and deposits posted to his account
D. amount of money left in Tu Nguyen's account based on his own calculations of the checks, charges, and deposits he has written and recorded

10. What of the following endorsements would be an example of a simple Endorsement in Blank? 10.____

A. Pay to the Order of Joanie Anderson
B. Joanie Anderson
C. For deposit only; Acct. No. 12345; Joanie Anderson
D. Without Recourse; Joanie Anderson

11. Which of the following endorsements would limit the further purpose or use of the endorsed check? 11.____

A. Pay to the Order of Joanie Anderson
B. Joanie Anderson
C. For deposit only; Acct. No. 12345; Joanie Anderson,
D. Without Recourse; Joanie Anderson

12. Which of the following endorsements would protect the endorser from legal responsibility for payment, should the drawer have insufficient funds to honor his/her own check? 12.____

A. Pay to the Order of Joanie Anderson
B. Joanie Anderson
C. For deposit only; Acct. No. 12345; Joanie Anderson
D. Without Recourse; Joanie Anderson

Questions 13-24.

DIRECTIONS: Questions 13 - 24 are to be answered on the basis of the following ledger accounts for Wheelsmith Organic Farms.

Wheelsmith Organic Farms
Ledger Accounts

Account	Debit	Credit
Cash	Jan. 1 4,000	
Accounts Payable		Jan. 1 2,000
Service Supplies	Jan. 1 2,000	
Shelley Wheelsmith, Capital		Jan. 1 11,000
Machinery	Jan. 1 7,000	

13. Transaction #1: On January 5, Shelley Wheelsmith, the proprietor, received cash amounting to $5,000 as a result of returning machinery that had recently been purchased. What account(s) should this transaction be posted to? 13.____

A. Cash
B. Cash and Machinery
C. Machinery
D. Cash, Machinery, and Service Supplies

14. Transaction #2: On January 8, Shelley Wheelsmith, the proprietor, sent out a check for $600 in partial payment of the accounts payable.
What account(s) should this transaction be posted to? 14.____

A. Accounts Payable
B. Accounts Payable and Cash
C. Accounts Payable and Capital
D. Cash

15. Transaction #3: On January 14, Shelley Wheelsmith, proprietor, made an additional investment in the business by contributing machinery valued at $1,500.
What account(s) should this transaction be posted to? 15.____

A. Machinery
B. Machinery and Capital
C. Capital
D. Machinery and Cash

16. Transaction #4: On January 26, Shelley Wheelsmith, proprietor, purchased additional service supplies for $200. She agreed to pay the obligation in 30 days. What account(s) should this transaction be posted to? 16.____

A. Accounts Payable and Liabilities
B. Service supplies
C. Accounts Payable
D. Accounts Payable and Service supplies

17. Transaction #5: On January 31, Shelley Wheelsmith, proprietor, purchased service supplies paying cash of $50. What account(s) should this transaction be posted to? 17.____

A. Service supplies
B. Service supplies and Accounts Payable
C. Cash and Service supplies
D. Cash

18. What is the balance in the Cash account after all of these transactions are posted? 18.____

A. $9,000 B. $1,000 C. $5,000 D. $8,350

19. What is the balance in the Machinery account after all of these transactions are posted? 19.____

A. $7,000 B. $5,000 C. $3,500 D. $13,500

20. What is the balance in the Accounts Payable account after all of these transactions are posted? 20.____

A. $800 B. $600 C. $2,600 D. $1,600

21. What is the balance in the Capital account after all of these transactions are posted? 21.____

A. $12,500 B. $800 C. $11,600 D. $10,400

22. What is the balance in the Service supplies account after all of these transactions are posted? 22.____

A. $2,000 B. $2,250 C. $750 D. $2,200

23. What are the total assets of Wheelsmith Organic Farms after these transactions have been posted? 23.____

A. $10,600 B. $11,850 C. $14,100 D. $10,750

24. What are the total liabilities and capital for Wheelsmith Organic Farms after these transactions have been posted? 24.____

A. $14,100 B. $12,500 C. $11,850 D. $10,600

Questions 25-28.

DIRECTIONS: Questions 25 through 28 are to be answered on the basis of the following information.

At the end of an accounting period, Andy's Framing Gallery recorded the following information: Sales, $125,225; Merchandise Inventory, December 31, $95,325; Purchases Returns and Allowances, $3,500; Merchandise Inventory, January 1, $98,725; Freight on Purchases, $2,500; Purchases, $120,000.

25. What are the net purchases for Andy's Framing Gallery during the accounting period? 25.____

A. $120,000 B. $119,000 C. $3,500 D. $122,500

26. What is the cost of goods available for sale? 26.____

A. $119,000 B. $98,725 C. $95,325 D. $217,725

27. What is the total cost of goods sold for this accounting period? 27.____

A. $217,725 B. $95,325 C. $122,400 D. $125,225

28. What is the gross profit on sales for this accounting period? 28.____

A. $2825 B. $2500 C. $125,225 D. $122,400

Questions 29-40.

DIRECTIONS: Questions 29 through 40 are to be answered on the basis of the following information.

The Joie de Vivre Co. received the promissory notes listed below during the last quarter of its calendar year:

	Date	Face Amount	Terms	Interest Rate	Date Discounted	Discount Rate
(1)	10/8	$3,600	30 days	-	10/18	9%
(2)	9/22	$8,000	60 days	6%	10/1	7%
(3)	11/15	$3,000	90 days	7%	11/20	8%

29. What is the due date for the first note? 29.____

A. 12/31 B. 11/7 C. 12/7 D. 10/31

30. What interest will be due when the first note matures? 30.____

A. $3 B. $3,600 C. $30 D. $0

31. What is the maturity value of the first note? 31.____

A. $3,600 B. $3,630 C. $0 D. $3,603

32. What is the discount period for the first note? 32.____

A. One fiscal year B. 10 days
C. 20 days D. One month

33. What is the due date for the second note? 33.____

A. 12/21 B. 11/21 C. 10/21 D. 1/21

34. What interest will be due when the second note matures? 34.____

A. $60 B. $800.00 C. $8.00 D. $80.00

35. What is the maturity value of the second note? 35.____

A. $8,000 B. $8,080 C. $8,800 D. $8,008

36. What is the discount period for the second note? 36.____

A. 51 days B. 10 days C. 360 days D. 60 days

37. What is the due date for the third note? 37.____

A. 1/14 B. 12/15 C. 12/31 D. 2/13

38. What interest will be due when the third note matures? 38.____

A. $5.25 B. $52.50 C. $525 D. $90

39. What is the maturity value of the third note? 39.____

A. $3525 B. $3005.25 C. $3052.50 D. $3090

40. What is the discount period for the third note? 40.____

A. 60 days B. 85 days C. 5 days D. 90 days

KEY (CORRECT ANSWERS)

1.	C	11.	C	21.	A	31.	A
2.	A	12.	D	22.	B	32.	C
3.	B	13.	B	23.	C	33.	B
4.	D	14.	B	24.	A	34.	D
5.	C	15.	B	25.	B	35.	B
6.	D	16.	D	26.	D	36.	A
7.	B	17.	C	27.	C	37.	D
8.	A	18.	D	28.	A	38.	B
9.	C	19.	C	29.	B	39.	C
10.	B	20.	D	30.	D	40.	B

TEST 3

DIRECTIONS: Each question or incomplete statement is followed by several suggested answers or completions. Select the one that BEST answers the question or completes the statement. *PRINT THE LETTER OF THE CORRECT ANSWER IN THE SPACE AT THE RIGHT.*

Questions 1-8.

DIRECTIONS: Questions 1 through 8 are to be answered on the basis of the following Balance Sheet.

Laura Lee's Bridal Shop
Balance Sheet
December 31, 2018

Assets		
Cash	$14,000	
Accounts Receivable	3,000	
Bridal Accessories	10,000	
Gowns and Other Inventory	30,000	
Total Assets		$57,000
Liabilities and Capital		
Accounts Payable	$ 4,000	
Notes Payable	28,000	
Total Liabilities		$32,000
Laura Lee, Capital		25,000
Total Liabilities and Capital		$57,000

1. When was the balance sheet prepared? 1.____

   A. January 2019
   B. December 31, 2018
   C. After the close of the 2018 fiscal year
   D. December 1, 2018

2. How does the date on this balance sheet differ from the date on the statement of capital or income statement? 2.____

   A. It doesn't differ. The dates for each statement signify the same time period.
   B. The date on a balance sheet represents the period during which any changes indicated on the statement took place, whereas the other financial statements represent the moment in time when the statement was prepared.
   C. The date on a balance sheet represents the moment in time when the statement was prepared, whereas the other financial statements represent the period during which any changes indicated on the statement took place.
   D. The date on a balance sheet indicates an entire year, whereas the dates on the other statements indicate a single month.

3. Can Laura Lee purchase more bridal gowns for the business paying cash of $16,000? 3.____

   A. *No*, because the business has only $14,000 cash available
   B. *Yes*, because the business has $57,000 cash available
   C. *Yes*, because the business has $57,000 available in assets
   D. *No*, because the business has $57,000 in liabilities

4. What is the owner's equity of Laura Lee's Bridal Shop? 4.____
Since total equity consists of total ______, total equity is ______.

A. assets minus total liabilities and proprietor's capital; $0
B. assets minus total liabilities; $25,000
C. assets; $57,000
D. liabilities and proprietor's capital; $57,000

5. What is the TOTAL amount of Laura Lee's claim against the total assets of the business? 5.____

A. $57,000 B. $25,000 C. $0 D. $39,000

6. What is the amount of the creditors' claims against the assets of the business? 6.____

A. $4,000 B. $57,000 C. $32,000 D. $28,000

7. What is the net income for the period? 7.____

A. $57,000
B. $0
C. $25,000
D. This information cannot be obtained from the balance sheet

8. What was the value of Laura Lee's ownership in this business on January 1, 2004? 8.____

A. $25,000
B. $57,000
C. $14,000
D. This information cannot be obtained from the balance sheet

Questions 9-21.

DIRECTIONS: Each of the transactions described in Questions 9 through 21 occurred within an accounting period. For each question, indicate which of the four journals the transaction would be recorded in.

9. Sale of goods on account 9.____

A. Cash receipts B. Cash payments
C. General D. Sales

10. Cash payment of a promissory note 10.____

A. Cash payments B. Cash receipts
C. Sales D. General

11. Received a credit memo from a creditor 11.____

A. Purchases B. General
C. Sales D. Cash payments

12. Sale of merchandise for cash 12.____

A. Purchases B. General
C. Cash receipts D. Cash payments

13. Received a check from a customer in partial payment of an oral agreement 13.____

A. Purchases
B. Sales
C. General
D. Cash receipts

14. Issued a credit memo to a customer 14.____

A. Purchases
B. General
C. Cash payments
D. Sales

15. Received a promissory note in place of an oral agreement from a customer 15.____

A. General
B. Cash payments
C. Cash receipts
D. Sales

16. Paid monthly rent 16.____

A. General
B. Purchases
C. Cash payments
D. Cash receipts

17. Sale of a service on credit 17.____

A. Cash receipts
B. General
C. Purchases
D. Sales

18. Purchase of office furniture on credit 18.____

A. General
B. Purchases
C. Cash payments
D. Cash receipts

19. Purchased merchandise for cash 19.____

A. Cash payments
B. Cash receipts
C. Sales
D. General

20. Cash refund to a customer 20.____

A. Cash receipts
B. Sales
C. General
D. Cash payments

21. Purchases made on credit 21.____

A. Purchases
B. Sales
C. Cash receipts
D. General

Questions 22-26.

DIRECTIONS: Questions 22 through 26 are to be answered on the basis of the following inventory, purchased by International Soap and Candle Traders, Inc.

700 units at $4.50, 320 units at $3.75, 550 units at $2.75, and 475 units at $1.90

22. Calculate the total price of the units that cost $4.50. 22.____

A. $315 B. $31,500 C. $3,150 D. $2,800

23. Calculate the total price of the units that cost $3.75. 23.____

A. $2062.50 B. $12,000 C. $120 D. $1,200

24. Calculate the total price of the units that cost $2.75. 24.____

A. $1,512.50 B. $15,125 C. $151.25 D. $550

25. Calculate the total price of the units that cost $1.90. 25.____

A. $90.25 B. $9025 C. $902.50 D. $475

26. Calculate the average cost per unit. 26.____

A. $27 B. $33.10 C. $0.30 D. $3.31

27. The interest on a promissory note is recorded at which of the following times? 27.____

A. When the debt is incurred
B. At the end of the accounting period
C. When the note is paid
D. At the beginning of each month

28. The interest on a promissory note begins accruing at which of the following times? 28.____

A. When the debt is incurred
B. At the end of the accounting period
C. When the note is paid
D. At the beginning of each month

29. The maturity value of an interest-bearing note is the 29.____

A. interest accrued on the note plus a service charge imposed by the lender
B. interest accrued on the note
C. face value of the note
D. principal of the note plus interest

30. A cash receipts journal is used to record the 30.____

A. number of cash sales a business makes
B. number of credit sales a business makes
C. collection of cash made by the business
D. expenditure of cash made by the business

31. Calculate the interest on a promissory note issued for $3,000 at an interest rate of 8%, due in 360 days. (Assume a banking year of 360 days.) 31.____

A. $300 B. $240 C. $60 D. $360

32. Calculate the total payment due for a promissory note issued for $1,000 at an interest rate of 10%, due in 90 days. (Assume a banking year of 360 days.) 32.____

A. $25 B. $1050 C. $1000 D. $1025

33. Calculate the total payment due for a promissory note issued for $5,000 at an interest rate of 6%, due in 60 days. (Assume a banking year of 360 days.) 33.____

A. $5,050 B. $50 C. $5,000 D. $5,300

34. Calculate the interest on a promissory note issued for $1,700 at an interest rate of 12%, due in 45 days. (Assume a banking year of 360 days.) 34.____

A. $204 B. $1725.50 C. $25.50 D. $1904

35. Calculate the interest on a promissory note issued for $600 at an interest rate of 9%, due in 90 days. (Assume a banking year of 360 days.) 35.____

A. $13.50 B. $135 C. $54 D. $540

KEY (CORRECT ANSWERS)

1.	B	16.	C
2.	C	17.	D
3.	A	18.	B
4.	B	19.	A
5.	B	20.	D
6.	C	21.	A
7.	D	22.	C
8.	D	23.	D
9.	D	24.	A
10.	A	25.	C
11.	B	26.	D
12.	C	27.	C
13.	D	28.	A
14.	B	29.	D
15.	A	30.	C

31.	B
32.	D
33.	A
34.	C
35.	A

EXAMINATION SECTION

TEST 1

DIRECTIONS: Each question or incomplete statement is followed by several suggested answers or completions. Select the one that BEST answers the question or completes the statement. *PRINT THE LETTER OF THE CORRECT ANSWER IN THE SPACE AT THE RIGHT.*

Questions 1-4.

DIRECTIONS: Questions 1 through 4 are to be answered SOLELY on the basis of the following passage.

Job analysis combined with performance appraisal is an excellent method of determining training needs of individuals. The steps in this method are to determine the specific duties of the job, to evaluate the adequacy with which the employee performs each of these duties, and finally to determine what significant improvements can be made by training.

The list of duties can be obtained in a number of ways: asking the employee, asking the supervisor, observing the employee, etc. Adequacy of performance can be estimated by the employee, but the supervisor's evaluation must also be obtained. This evaluation will usually be based on observation.

What does the supervisor observe? The employee, while he is working; the employee's work relationships; the ease, speed, and sureness of the employee's actions; the way he applies himself to the job; the accuracy and amount of completed work; its conformity with established procedures and standards; the appearance of the work; the soundness of judgment it shows; and, finally, signs of good or poor communication, understanding, and cooperation among employees.

Such observation is a normal and inseparable part of the everyday job of supervision. Systematically, recorded, evaluated, and summarized, it highlights both general and individual training needs.

1. According to the passage, job analysis may be used by the supervisor in 1.____
   A. increasing his own understanding of tasks performed in his unit
   B. increasing efficiency of communication within the organization
   C. assisting personnel experts in the classification of positions
   D. determining in which areas an employee needs more instruction

2. According to the passage, the FIRST step in determining the training needs of employees is to 2.____
   A. locate the significant improvements that can be made by training
   B. determine the specific duties required in a job
   C. evaluate the employee's performance
   D. motivate the employee to want to improve himself

3. On the basis of the above passage, which of the following is the BEST way for a supervisor to determine the adequacy of employee performance? 3.____
   A. Check the accuracy and amount of completed work
   B. Ask the training officer
   C. Observe all aspects of the employee's work
   D. Obtain the employee's own estimate

4. Which of the following is NOT mentioned by the passage as a factor to be taken into consideration in judging the adequacy of employee performance? 4.____
   A. Accuracy of completed work
   B. Appearance of completed work
   C. Cooperation among employees
   D. Attitude of the employee toward his supervisor

5. In indexing names of business firms and other organizations, ONE of the rules to be followed is: 5.____
   A. The word *and* is considered an indexing unit.
   B. When a firm name includes the full name of a person who is not well-known, the person's first name is considered as the first indexing unit.
   C. Usually the units in a firm name are indexed in the order in which they are written.
   D. When a firm's name is made up of single letters (such as ABC Corp.), the letters taken together are considered more than one indexing unit.

6. Assume that people often come to your office with complaints of errors in your agency's handling of their clients. The employees in your office have the job of listening to these complaints and investigating them. One day, when it is almost closing time, a person comes into your office, apparently very angry, and demands that you take care of his complaint at once. 6.____
   Your IMMEDIATE reaction should be to
   A. suggest that he return the following day
   B. find out his name and the nature of his complaint
   C. tell him to write a letter
   D. call over your supervisor

7. Assume that part of your job is to notify people concerning whether their applications for a certain program have been approved or disapproved. However, you do not actually make the decision on approval or disapproval. One day, you answer a telephone call from a woman who states that she has not yet received any word on her application. She goes on to tell you her qualifications for the program. From what she has said, you know that persons with such qualifications are usually approved. 7.____
   Of the following, which one is the BEST thing for you to say to her?
   A. "You probably will be accepted, but wait until you receive a letter before trying to join the program."
   B. "Since you seem well qualified, I am sure that your application will be approved."

C. "If you can write us a letter emphasizing your qualifications, it may speed up the process."
D. "You will be notified of the results of your application as soon as a decision has been made."

8. Suppose that one of your duties includes answering specific telephone inquiries. Your superior refers a call to you from an irate person who claims that your agency is inefficient and is wasting taxpayers' money. 8.____
Of the following, the BEST way to handle such a call is to
A. listen briefly and then hang up without answering
B. note the caller's comments and tell him that you will transmit them to your superiors
C. connect the caller with the head of your agency
D. discuss your own opinions with the caller

9. An employee has been assigned to open her division head's mail and place it on his desk. One day, the employee opens a letter which she then notices is marked *Personal.* 9.____
Of the following, the BEST action for her to take is to
A. write *Personal* on the letter and staple the envelope to the back of the letter
B. ignore the matter and treat the letter the same way as the others
C. give it to another division head to hold until her own division head comes into the office
D. leave the letter in the envelope and write *Sorry opened by mistake* on the envelope and initial it

Questions 10-14.

DIRECTIONS: Questions 10 through 14 each consist of a quotation which contains one word that is incorrectly used because it is not in keeping with the meaning that the quotation is evidently intended to convey. Of the words underlined in each quotation, determine which word is incorrectly used. Then select from among the words lettered A, B, C, and D the word which, when substituted for the incorrectly used word, would BEST help to convey the meaning of the quotation. (Do not indicate a change for an underlined word unless the underlined word is incorrectly used.)

10. Unless reasonable managerial supervision is <u>exercised</u> over office supplies, it is certain that there will be extravagance, <u>rejected</u> items out of stock, <u>excessive</u> prices paid for certain items, and <u>obsolete</u> material in the stockroom. 10.____
A. overlooked B. immoderate C. needed D. instituted

11. Since <u>office</u> supplies are in such <u>common</u> use, an attitude of indifference about their handling is not <u>unusual</u>. Their importance is often recognized only when they are <u>utilized</u> or out of stock, for office employees must have proper supplies if maximum productivity is to be <u>attained</u>. 11.____
A. plentiful B. unavailable C. reduced D. expected

12. Anyone effected by paperwork, interested in or engaged in office work, or desiring to improve informational activities can find materials keyed to his needs. 12.____
   A. attentive B. available C. affected D. ambitious

13. Information is homogeneous and must therefore be properly classified so that each type may be employed in ways appropriate to its own peculiar properties. 13.____
   A. apparent
   B. heterogeneous
   C. consistent
   D. idiosyncratic

14. Intellectual training may seem a formidable phrase, but it means nothing more than the deliberate cultivation of the ability to think, and there is no dark contrast between the intellectual and the practical. 14.____
   A. subjective B. objective C. sharp D. vocational

15. The MOST important reason for having a filing system is to 15.____
   A. get papers out of the way
   B. have a record of everything that has happened
   C. retain information to justify your actions
   D. enable rapid retrieval of information

16. The system of filing which is used MOST frequently is called _____ filing. 16.____
   A. alphabetic
   B. alphanumeric
   C. geographic
   D. numeric

17. One of the clerks under your supervision has been telephoning frequently to tell you that he was taking the day off. Unless there is a real need for it, taking leave which is not scheduled is frowned upon because it upsets the work schedule. 17.____
   Under these circumstances, which of the following reasons for taking the day off is MOST acceptable?
   A. "I can't work when my arthritis bothers me."
   B. "I've been pressured with work from my night job and needed the extra time to catch up."
   C. "My family just moved to a new house, and I needed the time to start the repairs."
   D. "Work here has not been challenging, and I've been looking for another job."

18. One of the employees under your supervision, previously a very satisfactory worker, has begun arriving late one or two mornings each week. No explanation has been offered for this change. You call her to your office for a conference. As you are explaining the purpose of the conference and your need to understand this sudden lateness problem, she becomes very angry and states that you have no right to question her. 18.____
   Of the following, the BEST course of action for you to take at this point is to

A. inform her in your most authoritarian tone that you are the supervisor and that you have every right to question her
B. end the conference and advise the employee that you will have no further discussion with her until she controls her temper
C. remain calm, try to calm her down, and when she has quieted, explain the reasons for your questions and the need for answers
D. hold your temper; when she has calmed down, tell her that you will not have a tardy worker in your unit and will have her transferred at once

19. Assume that, in the branch of the agency for which you work, you are the only clerical person on the staff with a supervisory title and, in addition, that you are the office manager. On a particular day when all members of the professional staff are away from the building attending an important meeting, an urgent call comes through requesting some confidential information ordinarily released only by professional staff. 19.____
Of the following, the MOST reasonable action for you to take is to
A. decline to give the information because you are not a member of the professional staff
B. offer to call back after you get permission from the agency director at the main office
C. advise the caller that you will supply the information as soon as your chief returns
D. supply the information requested and inform your chief when she returns

20. As a supervisor, you are scheduled to attend an important conference with your superior. However, that day you learn that your very capable assistant is ill and unable to come to work. Several highly sensitive tasks are scheduled for completion on this day. 20.____
Of the following, the BEST way to handle this situation is to
A. tell your supervisor you cannot attend the meeting and ask that it be postponed
B. assign one of your staff to see that the jobs are completed and turned in
C. advise your supervisor of the situation and ask what you should do
D. call the departments for which the work is being done and ask for an extension of time

21. When a decision needs to be made which is likely to affect units other than his own, a supervisor should USUALLY 21.____
A. make such a decision quickly and then discuss it with his supervisor
B. make such a decision only after careful consultation with his subordinates
C. discuss the problem with his immediate superior before making such a decision
D. have his subordinates arrive at such a decision in conference with the subordinates in the other units

22. Assume that, as a supervisor in Division X, you are training Ms. Y, a new employee, to answer the telephone properly. 22.____
You should explain that the BEST way to answer is to pick up the receiver and say:

A. "What is your name, please?"
B. "May I help you?"
C. "Ms. Y speaking."
D. "Division X, Ms. Y speaking."

Questions 23-25.

DIRECTIONS: Questions 23 through 25 consist of sentences in which two words are missing. Examine each sentence, and then choose from below it the words which should be inserted in the blank spaces in order to create a coherent and well-written sentence.

23. Human behavior is far _____ variable, and therefore _____ predictable, than that of any other species. 23.____
A. less; as
B. less; not
C. more; not
D. more; less

24. The _____ limitation of this method is that the results are based _____ a narrow sample. 24.____
A. chief; with
B. chief; on
C. only; for
D. only; to

25. Although there _____ a standard procedure for handling these problems, each case often has _____ own unique features. 25.____
A. are; its
B. are; their
C. is; its
D. is; their

KEY (CORRECT ANSWERS)

1.	D	11.	B
2.	B	12.	C
3.	C	13.	B
4.	D	14.	C
5.	C	15.	D
6.	B	16.	A
7.	D	17.	A
8.	B	18.	C
9.	D	19.	B
10.	C	20.	C

21. C
22. D
23. D
24. B
25. C

TEST 2

DIRECTIONS: Each question or incomplete statement is followed by several suggested answers or completions. Select the one that BEST answers the question or completes the statement. *PRINT THE LETTER OF THE CORRECT ANSWER IN THE SPACE AT THE RIGHT.*

Questions 1-3.

DIRECTIONS: Questions 1 through 3 each consist of a group of four sentences. Read each sentence carefully, and select the one of the four in each group which represents the BEST English usage for business letters and reports.

1. A. The chairman himself, rather than his aides, has reviewed the report. 1.____
   B. The chairman himself, rather than his aides, have reviewed the report.
   C. The chairmen, not the aide, has reviewed the report.
   D. The aide, not the chairmen, have reviewed the report.

2. A. Various proposals were submitted but the decision is not been made. 2.____
   B. Various proposals has been submitted but the decision has not been made.
   C. Various proposals were submitted but the decision is not been made.
   D. Various proposals have been submitted but the decision has not been made.

3. A. Everyone were rewarded for his successful attempt. 3.____
   B. They were successful in their attempts and each of them was rewarded.
   C. Each of them are rewarded for their successful attempts.
   D. The reward for their successful attempts were made to each of them.

4. Which of the following is MOST suited to arrangement in chronological order? 4.____
   A. Applications for various types and levels of jobs
   B. Issues of a weekly publication
   C. Weekly time cards for all employees for the week of April 21
   D. Personnel records for all employees

5. Words that are *synonymous* with a given word ALWAYS _____ the given word. 5.____
   A. have the same meaning as
   B. have the same pronunciation as
   C. have the opposite meaning of
   D. can be rhymed with

Questions 6-11.

DIRECTIONS: Questions 6 through 11 are to be answered on the basis of the following chart showing numbers of errors made by four clerks in one work unit for a half-year period.

	Allan	Barry	Cary	David
July	5	4	1	7
August	8	3	9	8
September	7	8	7	5
October	3	6	5	3
November	2	4	4	6
December	5	2	8	4

6. The clerk with the HIGHEST number of errors for the six-month period was 6.____
   A. Allan B. Barry C. Cary D. David

7. If the number of errors made by Allan in the six months shown represented one-eighth of the total errors made by the unit during the entire year, what was the TOTAL number of errors made by the unit for the year? 7.____
   A. 124 B. 180 C. 240 D. 360

8. The number of errors made by David in November was what FRACTION of the total errors made in November? 8.____
   A. 1/3 B. 1/6 C. 3/8 D. 3/16

9. The average number of errors made per month per clerk was MOST NEARLY 9.____
   A. 4 B. 5 C. 6 D. 7

10. Of the total number of errors made during the six-month period, the percentage made in August was MOST NEARLY 10.____
    A. 2% B. 4% C. 23% D. 4%

11. If the number of errors in the unit were to decrease in the next six months by 30%, what would be MOST NEARLY the total number of errors for the unit for the next six months? 11.____
    A. 87 B. 94 C. 120 D. 137

12. The arithmetic mean salary for five employees earning $18,500, $18,300, $18,600, $18,400, and $18,500, respectively is 12.____
    A. $18,450 B. $18,460 C. $18,475 D. $18,500

13. Last year, a city department which is responsible for purchasing supplies ordered bond paper in equal quantities from 22 different companies. The price was exactly the same for each company, and the total cost for the 22 orders was $693,113. 13.____
    Assuming prices did not change during the year, the cost of EACH order was MOST NEARLY
    A. $31,490 B. $31,495 C. $31,500 D. $31,505

14. A city agency engaged in repair work uses a small part which the city purchases for $0.14 each. Assume that, in a certain year, the total expenditure of the city for this part was $700. 14.____
How MANY of these parts were purchased that year?
A. 50 B. 200 C. 2,000 D. 5,000

15. The work unit which you supervise is responsible for processing fifteen reports per month. 15.____
If your unit has four clerks and the best worker completes 40% of the reports himself, how many reports would each of the other clerks have to complete if they all do an equal number?
A. 1 B. 2 C. 3 D. 4

16. Assume that the work unit in which you work has 24 clerks and 18 stenographers. 16.____
In order to change the ratio of stenographers to clerks so that there is one stenographer for every four clerks, it would be necessary to REDUCE the number of stenographers by
A. 3 B. 6 C. 9 D. 12

17. Assume that your office is responsible for opening and distributing all the mail of the division. After opening a letter, one of your subordinates notices that it states that there should be an enclosure in the envelope. However, there is no enclosure in the envelope. 17.____
Of the following, the BEST instruction that you can give the clerk is to
A. call the sender to obtain the enclosure
B. call the addressee to inform him that the enclosure is missing
C. note the omission in the margin of the letter
D. forward the letter without taking any action

18. While opening the envelope containing official correspondence, you accidentally cut the enclosed letter. 18.____
Of the following, the BEST action for you to take is to
A. leave the material as it is
B. put it together by using transparent mending tape
C. keep it together by putting it back in the envelope
D. keep it together by using paper clips

19. Suppose your supervisor is on the telephone in his office and an applicant arrives for a scheduled interview with him. 19.____
Of the following, the BEST procedure to follow ordinarily is to
A. informally chat with the applicant in your office until your supervisor has finished his phone conversation
B. escort him directly into your supervisor's office and have him wait for him there
C. inform your supervisor of the applicant's arrival and try to make the applicant feel comfortable while waiting
D. have him hang up his coat and tell him to go directly in to see your supervisor

20. The length of time that files should be kept is GENERALLY 20.____
    A. considered to be seven years
    B. dependent upon how much new material has accumulated in the files
    C. directly proportionate to the number of years the office has been in operation
    D. dependent upon the type and nature of the material in the files

21. Cross-referencing a document when you file it means 21.____
    A. making a copy of the document and putting the copy into a related file
    B. indicating on the front of the document the name of the person who wrote it, the date it was written, and for what purpose
    C. putting a special sheet or card in a related file to indicate where the document is filed
    D. indicating on the document where it is to be filed

22. Unnecessary handling and recording of incoming mail could be eliminated by 22.____
    A. having the person who opens it initial it
    B. indicating on the piece of mail the names of all the individuals who should see it
    C. sending all incoming mail to more than one central location
    D. making a photocopy of each piece of incoming mail

23. Of the following, the office tasks which lend themselves MOST readily to planning and study are 23.____
    A. repetitive, occur in volume, and extend over a period of time
    B. cyclical in nature, have small volume, and extend over a short period of time
    C. tasks which occur only once in a great while not according to any schedule, and have large volume
    D. special tasks which occur only once, regardless of their volume and length of time

24. A good recordkeeping system includes all of the following procedures EXCEPT the 24.____
    A. filing of useless records
    B. destruction of certain files
    C. transferring of records from one type of file to another
    D. creation of inactive files

25. Assume that, as a supervisor, you are responsible for orienting and training new employees in your unit. 25.____
    Which of the following can MOST properly be omitted from your discussions with a new employee?
    A. The purpose of commonly used office forms
    B. Time and leave regulations
    C. Procedures for required handling of routine business calls
    D. The reason the last employee was fired

KEY (CORRECT ANSWERS)

1.	A	11.	A
2.	D	12.	B
3.	B	13.	D
4.	B	14.	D
5.	A	15.	C
6.	C	16.	D
7.	C	17.	C
8.	C	18.	B
9.	B	19.	C
10.	C	20.	D

21. C
22. B
23. A
24. A
25. D

EXAMINATION SECTION
TEST 1

DIRECTIONS: Each question or incomplete statement is followed by several suggested answers or completions. Select the one that BEST answers the question or completes the statement. *PRINT THE LETTER OF THE CORRECT ANSWER IN THE SPACE AT THE RIGHT.*

1. You have recently been assigned to a new office and are expected to supervise six clerks. 1.____
All of the following would be good introductory steps to take EXCEPT

    A. giving a clear presentation of yourself to the clerks, including a short summary of your recent work experience
    B. initiating informal discussions with each clerk concerning his work
    C. making a general survey of all the functions which each clerk has been performing
    D. making a list of the duties each clerk is required to perform and giving it to the clerk

2. Your supervisor has advised you that a specific aspect of a job is being done incorrectly and you acknowledge the mistake. 2.____
Of the following, the MOST efficient way of dealing with this situation is to

    A. call a meeting of the clerks who are performing this particular function and explain the correct method
    B. assume the blame and correct the errors as they are given to you
    C. speak with each clerk individually and carefully show each one the proper method
    D. distribute a set of written instructions covering all clerical procedures to the employees doing that particular job

3. A new department regulation calls for a change in a particular method of processing new applications. Two clerks have complained to you that the new method is more time-consuming, and they prefer to do it the original way. 3.____
Of the following, what is the MOST advisable thing to do?

    A. Discuss the situation with them and attempt to determine whether they are utilizing the method properly.
    B. Discuss the advantages of both methods with them and let them use the one that is more practical.
    C. Firmly instruct the clerks to proceed with the new method since it is not up to them to refute department policy.
    D. Tell them to survey the opinions of the other clerks on this matter and inform you of the results.

4. A member of the clerical staff has recently begun reporting late for work rather regularly. On each occasion, the individual presented an excuse, but the latenesses continue. 4.____
Of the following, the MOST advisable action for her supervisor to take is to

    A. have a staff meeting and stress the importance of being on time for work, without singling out the specific individual
    B. put a notice on the departmental office bulletin board, specifying and stressing that lateness can not be tolerated

C. talk privately with the individual to determine whether theré are any unusual circumstances that might be causing the lateness
D. send the individual a memorandum clearly indicating that continual lateness will result in disciplinary action

5. Assume that, as the supervisor of a unit, you have been asked to prepare a vacation schedule for your subordinate employees. The employees have had different lengths of service. Some of them have already submitted requests for certain weeks. 5.____
Of the following, which factor would be LEAST important in setting up this schedule?

A. Your opinion of each employee's past work performance
B. Each employee's preference for a vacation period
C. The amount of work the unit is expected to accomplish during the vacation period
D. The number of employees who have requested to go on vacation at the same time

6. Your superior finds that he must leave the office one day before he has had time to check and sign the day's correspondence. He asks you to proofread the letters, have corrections made where necessary, and then sign his name. You have never signed his name before. 6.____
Of the following, the BEST thing for you to do is to

A. sign your superior's name in full, making it look as much like his handwriting as possible
B. sign your superior's name and your own name in full as proof that you signed for him
C. sign your superior's name in full and add your initials to show that the signature is not his own
D. politely refuse to sign his name because it is forgery

7. The head of your office sometimes makes handwritten notations on original letters which he receives and requests that you mail the letters back to the sender. Of the following, the BEST action for you to take FIRST is to 7.____

A. request that this practice be stopped because it does not provide for a record in the files
B. request that this practice be stopped because it is not the customary way to respond to letters
C. photocopy the letters so that there are copies for the file and then send the letters out
D. ask the head of your office if he wants you to keep any record of the letters

8. The main function of most agency administrative offices is *information management.* Information that is received by an administrative office may be classified as active (information which requires the recipient to take some action) or passive (information which does not require action). 8.____
Which one of the following items received must clearly be treated as ACTIVE information?
A(n)

A. confirmation of payment
B. press release concerning an agency event
C. advertisement for a new restaurant opening near the agency
D. request for a student transcript

9. Which of the following statements about the use of the photocopy process is CORRECT? 9.____

   A. It is difficult to use.
   B. It can be used to reproduce color.
   C. It does not print well on colored paper.
   D. Once source documents have been used, they cannot be used again.

10. In order to get the BEST estimate of how long a repetitive office procedure should take, a supervisor should find out how 10.____

    A. long it takes her best worker to do the procedure once on a typical day
    B. long it takes her best and worst workers to do the procedure once on a typical day
    C. much time her best worker spends on the procedure during a typical week and the total number of times the worker executes the procedure during the same week
    D. much time all her subordinates spend on the procedure during a typical week and the total number of times the procedure was executed during the same week by all employees

11. Of the following, the MOST suitable and appropriate way to make 250 copies of a particular form is to 11.____

    A. print all 250 copies on the office computer
    B. delegate the work to someone else
    C. reproduce it on a photocopying machine
    D. use an offset printing process

Questions 12-18.

DIRECTIONS: Questions 12 through 18 are to be answered on the basis of the extracts shown below from Federal withholding tables. These tables indicate the amounts which must be withheld from the employee's salary by his employer for Federal income tax and for social security. They are based on weekly earnings.

INCOME TAX WITHHOLDING TABLE

The wages are -		And the number of withholding exemptions claimed is-					
At least	But less than	0	1	2	3	4	5
		The amount of income tax to be withheld shall be -					
$200	$205	$14.10	$11.80	$ 9.50	$ 7.20	$ 4.90	$2.80
205	210	14.90	12.60	10.30	8.00	5.70	3.50
210	215	15.70	13.40	11.10	8.80	6.50	4.20
215	220	16.50	14.20	11.90	9.60	7.30	5.00
220	225	17.30	15.00	12.70	10.40	8.10	5.80
225	230	18.10	15.80	13.50	11.20	8.90	6.60
230	235	18.90	16.60	14.30	12.00	9.70	7.40
235	240	19.70	17.40	15.10	12.80	10.50	8.20
240	245	20.50	18.20	15.90	13.60	11.30	9.00
245	250	21.30	19.00	16.70	14.40	12.10	9.80

SOCIAL SECURITY EMPLOYEE TAX TABLE

Wages		Tax to be withheld	Wages		Tax to be withheld
At least	But less than		At least	But less than	
$202.79	$202.99	$15.35	$229.72	$229.91	$16.75
202.99	203.18	15.36	229.91	230.10	16.76
203.18	203.37	15.37	230.10	230.29	16.77
203.37	203.56	15.38	230.29	230.49	16.78
203.56	203.75	15.39	230.49	230.68	16.79
203.75	203.95	15.40	230.68	230.87	16.80
203.95	204.14	15.41	230.87	231.06	16.81
204.14	204.33	15.42	231.06	231.25	16.82
204.33	204.52	15.43	231.25	231.45	16.83
204.52	204.72	15.44	231.45	231.64	16.84

Wages		Tax to be withheld	Wages		Tax to be withheld
At least	But less than		At least	But less than	
$222.02	$222.22	$16.35	$234.52	$234.72	$17.00
222.22	222.41	16.36	234.72	234.91	17.01
222.41	222.60	16.37	234.91	235.10	17.02
222.60	222.79	16.38	235.10	235.29	17.03
222.79	222.99	16.39	235.29	235.49	17.04
222.99	223.18	16.40	235.49	235.68	17.05
223.18	223.37	16.41	235.68	235.87	17.06
223.37	223.56	16.42	235.87	236.06	17.07
223.56	223.75	16.43	236.06	236.25	17.08
223.75	223.95	16.44	236.25	236.45	17.09

12. Dave Andes has wages of $242.75 for one week. He has claimed three withholding exemptions. 12.____
What is the Federal income tax which should be withheld?

A. $13.60 B. $15.90 C. $18.20 D. $20.50

13. Mary Hodes has wages of $229.95 for one week. 13.____
What is the Social Security tax which should be withheld?

A. $16.75 B. $16.76 C. $16.77 D. $16.78

14. Joe Jones had wages of $235.63 for one week. He has claimed two withholding exemptions. 14.____
What is the Federal income tax which should be withheld?

A. $12.80 B. $14.30 C. $15.10 D. $17.40

15. Tom Stein had wages of $203.95 for one week. What is the Social Security tax which should be withheld? 15.____

A. $15.40 B. $15.41 C. $16.05 D. $16.06

16. Robert Helman had wages of $222.80 for one week. He has claimed one withholding exemption. 16.____
If only Federal income tax and Social Security tax were deducted from his earnings for the same week, how much *take-home* pay should he have for the week?

A. $191.41 B. $193.96 C. $194.12 D. $195.65

17. Audrey Stein has wages of $203.00 for one week. She claimed no withholding exemptions. 17.____
If only Federal income tax and Social Security tax were deducted from her earnings for the same week, how much *take-home* pay should she have for the week?

A. $171.84 B. $172.34 C. $173.54 D. $175.84

18. Anthony Covallo, who worked 28 hours in the past week, has a regular hourly rate of $7.25 per hour and earns a premium of time and a half for hours over 40. He has claimed four withholding exemptions. 18.____
After Social Security tax and Federal income tax are deducted from his wages for the past week, how much pay does he have left?

A. $180.98 B. $181.13 C. $182.29 D. $182.74

19. In judging the adequacy of a standard office form, which of the following is LEAST important? 19.____
_______ of the form.

A. Date B. Legibility C. Size D. Design

20. Clear and accurate telephone messages should be taken for employees who are out of the office. 20.____
Which of the following is of LEAST importance when taking a telephone message?

A. Name of the person called
B. Name of the caller

C. Details of the message
D. Time of the call

21. Suppose that all office supplies are kept in a centrally located cabinet in the office. Of the following, which is usually the BEST policy to adhere to for distribution of supplies? 21.____

A. Permit employees to stock up on all supplies to avoid frequent trips to the cabinet.
B. Assign one employee to be in charge of distributing all supplies to other employees at frequent intervals.
C. Inform employees that supplies should be taken in large quantities and only when needed.
D. Keep cabinet closed and instruct employees that they must check with you before taking supplies.

Questions 22-25.

DIRECTIONS: Questions 22 through 25 are to be answered SOLELY on the basis of the following passage.

Use of the systems and procedures approach to office management is revolutionizing the supervision of office work. This approach views an enterprise as an entity which seeks to fulfill definite objectives. Systems and procedures help to organize repetitive work into a routine, thus reducing the amount of decision-making required for its accomplishment. As a result, employees are guided in their efforts and perform only necessary work. Supervisors are relieved of any details of execution and are free to attend to more important work. Establishing work guides which require that identical tasks be performed the same way each, time permits standardization of forms, machine operations, work methods, and controls. This approach also reduces the probability of errors. Any error committed is usually discovered quickly because the incorrect work does not meet the requirement of the work guides. Errors are also reduced through work specialization which allows each employee to become thoroughly proficient in a particular type of work. Such proficiency also tends to improve the morale of the employees.

22. Of the following, which one BEST expresses the main theme of the above passage? The 22.____

A. advantages and disadvantages of the systems and procedures approach to office management
B. effectiveness of the systems and procedures approach to office management in developing skills
C. systems and procedures approach to office management as it relates to office costs
D. advantages of the systems and procedures approach to office management for supervisors and office workers

23. Work guides are LEAST likely to be used when 23.____

A. standardized forms are used
B. a particular office task is distinct and different from all others
C. identical tasks are to be performed in identical ways
D. similar work methods are expected from each employee

24. According to the above passage, when an employee makes a work error, it USUALLY 24.____
    A. is quickly corrected by the supervisor
    B. necessitates a change in the work guides
    C. can be detected quickly if work guides are in use
    D. increases the probability of further errors by that employee

25. The above passage states that the accuracy of an employee's work is INCREASED by 25.____
    A. using the work specialization approach
    B. employing a probability sample
    C. requiring him to shift at one time into different types of tasks
    D. having his supervisor check each detail of work execution

---

KEY (CORRECT ANSWERS)

1.	D	11.	C
2.	A	12.	A
3.	A	13.	B
4.	C	14.	C
5.	A	15.	B
6.	C	16.	A
7.	D	17.	C
8.	D	18.	D
9.	B	19.	A
10.	D	20.	D

21.	B
22.	D
23.	B
24.	C
25.	A

TEST 2

DIRECTIONS: Each question or incomplete statement is followed by several suggested answers or completions. Select the one that BEST answers the question or completes the statement. *PRINT THE LETTER OF THE CORRECT ANSWER IN THE SPACE AT THE RIGHT.*

1. A certain supervisor often holds group meetings with subordinates to discuss the goals of the unit and manpower requirements for meeting objectives. 1.____
For the supervisor to hold such meetings is a

   A. *good* practice because it will aid both the supervisor and subordinates in planning and completing the unit's work
   B. *good* practice because it will prevent future problems from interfering with the unit's objectives
   C. *poor* practice because the supervisor has the sole responsibility for meeting objectives and should make manpower decisions without any advice
   D. *poor* practice because the subordinates will be allowed to set their own work quotas

2. Assume that you are a supervisor who has been asked to evaluate the work of a clerk who was transferred to your unit about six months ago. 2.____
Which one of the following, by itself, provides the BEST basis for making such an evaluation?

   A. Ask the clerk's former supervisor about the employee's previous work.
   B. Ask the clerk's co-workers for their opinions of the employee's work.
   C. Evaluate the quantity and quality of the employee's work over the six-month period.
   D. Observe the employee's performance from time to time during the next week and base your evaluation on these observations.

3. Which of the following would be the MOST desirable way for a supervisor to help improve the job performance of a particular subordinate? 3.____

   A. Criticize the employee's performance in front of other employees.
   B. Privately warn the employee that failure to meet work standards may lead to dismissal.
   C. Hold a meeting with this employee and other subordinates in which the need to improve the unit's performance is stressed.
   D. Meet privately with the employee and discuss both positive and negative aspects of the employee's work

4. Suppose that your office has a limited supply of a pamphlet which people may read in your office when they seek certain information, but another office in your building is supposed to have a large supply available for distribution to the public. 4.____
Which of the following would be the BEST thing for you to do when someone states that he has not been able to obtain one of these pamphlets?

   A. Tell him that he misunderstood the directions that other employees have given him and carefully direct him to the other office.
   B. Ask whether he has visited the other office and requested a copy from them.
   C. Let him take one of your office's copies of the pamphlet and then call the other office and ask why they have run out of copies for distribution.

D. Tell him that your office does its best to keep the public informed but that this might not be true of other offices.

5. On Monday, a clerk made many errors in completing a new daily record form. The supervisor explained the errors and had the clerk correct the form. On Tuesday, the clerk made fewer errors. Because he was very busy, the supervisor did not point out the errors to the clerk but corrected the errors himself. On Wednesday, the clerk made the same number of errors as on Tuesday. The supervisor reprimanded the clerk for making so many errors. 5.____
The supervisor's handling of this situation on Wednesday may be considered poor MAINLY because the

A. clerk was not given enough time to complete each form properly
B. supervisor should not have expected improvement without further training
C. clerk was obviously incapable of completing the form
D. supervisor should have continued to correct the errors himself

Questions 6-8.

DIRECTIONS: Questions 6 through 8 are to be answered SOLELY on the basis of the information contained in the following passage.

When using words like company, association, *council, committee, and board in place of the full official name, the writer should not capitalize these short forms unless he intends them to invoke the full force of the institution's authority. In legal contracts, in minutes, or in formal correspondence where one is speaking formally and officially on behalf of the company, the term "Company" is usually capitalized, but in ordinary usage, where it is not essential to load the short form with this significance, capitalization would be excessive. (Example: The company will have many good openings for graduates this June.)*

The treatment recommended for short forms of place names is essentially the same as that recommended for short forms of organizational names. In general, we capitalize the full form but not the short form. If Park Avenue is referred to in one sentence, then "the avenue" is sufficient in subsequent references. The same is true with words like building, hotel, station, and airport, which are capitalized when part of a proper name (Pan Am Building, Hotel Plaza, Union Station, O'Hare Airport) but are simply lower-cased when replacing these specific names.

6. The above passage states that USUALLY the short forms of names of organizations 6.____

A. and places should not be capitalized
B. and places should be capitalized
C. should not be capitalized, but the short forms of names of places should be capitalized
D. should be capitalized, but the short forms of names of places should not be capitalized

7. The above passage states that in legal contracts, in minutes, and in formal correspondence, the short forms of names of organizations should 7.____

A. usually not be capitalized
B. usually be capitalized
C. usually not be used
D. never be used

8. It can be INFERRED from the above passage that decisions regarding when to capitalize certain words 8.____

   A. should be left to the discretion of the writer
   B. should be based on generally accepted rules
   C. depend on the total number of words capitalized
   D. are of minor importance

9. The Central Terminal and the Gardens Terminal are located on Glover Street. 9.____
   In ordinary usage, if this sentence were to be followed by the sentence in the choices below, which form of the sentence would be CORRECT?

   A. Both Terminals are situated on the same street.
   B. Both terminals are situated on the same Street.
   C. Both terminals are situated on the same street.
   D. Both Terminals are situated on the same Street.

10. A stylus is a(n) 10.____

   A. implement for writing containing a cylinder of graphite
   B. implement for writing with ink or a similar fluid
   C. pointed implement used to write
   D. stick of colored wax used for writing

11. As a supervisor, you have the responsibility of teaching new employees the functions and procedures of your office after their orientation by the personnel office. 11.____
   Of the following, the BEST way to begin such instruction is to

   A. advise the new employee of the benefits and services available to him, over and above his salary
   B. discuss the negative aspects of the departmental procedures and indicate methods available to overcome them
   C. assist the new employee in understanding the general purpose of the office procedures and how they fit in with the overall operation
   D. give a detailed briefing of the operations of your office, its functions and procedures

12. Assume that you are the supervisor of a clerical unit. One of the duties of the employees in your unit is to conduct a brief interview with persons using the services of your agency for the first time. The purpose of the interview is to get general background information in order to best direct them to the appropriate division. 12.____
   A clerk comes to your office and says that a prospective client has just called her some rather unpleasant names, accused her of being nosey and meddlesome, and has stated emphatically that she refuses to talk with an *underling,* meaning the clerk. The young woman is almost in tears. Of the following, what is the FIRST action you should take?

   A. Immediately call the agency's protection officer, have him advise the client of the regulations, and tell her that she will be removed if she is not more polite.
   B. Calm the clerk, introduce yourself to the client, and quietly discuss the agency's services, regulations, and informational needs, and request that she complete the interview with the clerk.

C. Calm the clerk, have her return and firmly advise the client of the agency's rules concerning the need for this first interview.
D. Introduce yourself to the client and advise her that without an apology to the clerk and completion of the interview, she will not be given any service.

13. A recent high school graduate has just been assigned to the unit which you supervise. Which of the following would be the LEAST desirable technique to use with this employee? 13.____

A. At any one time, give the new employee only as much detail about the job as the employee can absorb.
B. Always tell the new employee the correct procedure, then demonstrate how it is accomplished.
C. Assign the employee the same quantity and type of work that the other employees are doing to see if the employee can handle the job.
D. Assume the employee is tense and be prepared to repeat procedures and descriptions.

14. Assume that you supervise a work unit of several employees. Which of the following is LEAST essential in assuring that the goals which you set for the unit are achieved? 14.____

A. Establishing objectives and standards for the staff
B. Providing justification for disciplinary action
C. Measuring performance or progress of individuals against standards
D. Taking corrective action where performance is less than expected

15. One of the clerks you supervise is often reluctant to accept assignments and usually complains about the amount of work expected, although the other clerks with the same assignments and workload seem quite happy.
Of the following, the MOST accurate assumption that you can make about this clerk is that she 15.____

A. will require additional observation and help
B. will eventually have to be discharged or transferred
C. is incompetent
D. is overworked

Questions 16-21.

DIRECTIONS: Questions 16 through 21 are to be answered SOLELY on the basis of the airline timetable and the information appearing on the last page of this test.

Fact Situation:

An administrator wants you to purchase airline tickets for him so that he can attend a meeting being held in Chicago on Monday. He must leave from LaGuardia Airport in New York on Monday morning as late as possible but with arrival in Chicago no later than 9:00 A.M. He wishes to fly coach/economy class both ways. The meeting is due to end at 5:30 P.M., and he wishes to obtain the first plane after 6:45 P.M. going back to LaGuardia Airport. If all these requirements have been met, he would, if possible, also like to fly to and leave from Midway Airport in Chicago and go non-stop both ways.

16. You should obtain a ticket for the administrator from New York to Chicago on flight number 16.____

A. 483 B. 201 C. 277 D. 539

17. You should obtain a ticket for the administrator from Chicago to New York on flight number 17.____

A. 588 B. 692 C. 268 D. 334

18. The administrator decides to take limousines to and from both airports. 18.____
If the limousine charge in Chicago is $52.50. and there is no reduced rate for a round-trip flight, what is the cost of the administrator's round-trip air fare PLUS limousine service?

A. $827.50 B. $931.00 C. $963.00 D. $967.00

19. The administrator asked you whether he would be able to get breakfast on his flight to Chicago or whether he should go to the airport early and eat there before boarding the plane. He prefers to eat on the plane. 19.____
Of the following, the BEST reply to make is:

A. I will have to telephone the airport to find out
B. You should eat at the airport
C. A meal is served on the plane
D. Only certain passengers get a meal on the plane

20. Of the following requests of the administrator concerning his travel arrangements, which one is IMPOSSIBLE to meet? 20.____

A. Chicago arrival no later than 9 A.M.
B. New York departure from LaGuardia Airport
C. Non-stop flights both ways
D. Chicago departure from Midway Airport

21. Suppose that it is necessary to take a first-class seat on the trip to Chicago although you have no problem reserving a coach/economy seat on the return trip. 21.____
If there is no reduction in fare for round-trip flights, how much MORE will this trip cost than round-trip coach/ economy?

A. $209 B. $236 C. $318 D. $636

22. Ms. X, a clerk under your supervision, has been working in the unit for a few weeks. Some of the other employees have complained to you that Ms. X has an annoying habit of constantly tapping her feet on the floor and it disturbs their work. 22.____
The BEST thing for you to do is to

A. ignore the complaints because the employees should be concerned only with their own habits
B. speak with Ms. X privately and discuss the situation with her
C. make a general announcement that employees should control their nervous habits
D. observe Ms. X for a few weeks to see if the employees are correct, and then take action

23. Suppose you answer a telephone call from someone who states that he is a friend of one of your co-workers and needs the employee's new address in order to send an invitation. Your co-worker is on vacation but you know her address. Which of the following is the BEST action for you to take? 23.____

A. Give the caller the address but ask the caller not to mention that you are the one who gave it out.
B. Give the caller the address and leave a note for your co-worker stating what you did.
C. Tell the caller you do not know the address but will give the employee's phone number if that will help.
D. Offer to take his name and address and have your co-worker contact him.

24. Assume that you receive a telephone call in which the caller requests information which you know is posted in the office next to yours. You start to tell the caller you will transfer her call to the right office, but she interrupts you and says she has been transferred from office to office and is tired of getting a *run-around*. Of the following, the BEST thing for you to do is to 24.____

A. give the caller the phone number of the office next to yours and quickly end the conversation
B. give her the phone number of the office next to yours and tell her you will try to transfer her call
C. ask her if she wants to hold on while you get the information for her
D. tell the caller that she could have avoided the *run-around* by asking for the right office, and suggest that she come in person

25. Assume that your unit processes confidential forms which are submitted by persons seeking financial assistance. An individual comes to your office, gives you his name, and states that he would like to look over a form which he sent in about a week ago because he believes he omitted some important information. Of the following, the BEST thing for you to do FIRST is to 25.____

A. locate the proper form
B. call the individual's home telephone number to verify his identity
C. ask the individual if he has proof of his identity
D. call the security office

KEY (CORRECT ANSWERS)

1. A
2. C
3. D
4. B
5. B
6. A
7. B
8. B
9. C
10. C
11. C
12. B
13. C
14. B
15. A
16. A
17. D
18. B
19. C
20. D
21. C
22. B
23. D
24. C
25. C

EXAMINATION SECTION

TEST 1

DIRECTIONS: Each question or incomplete statement is followed by several suggested answers or completions. Select the one that BEST answers the question or completes the statement. *PRINT THE LETTER OF THE CORRECT ANSWER IN THE SPACE AT THE RIGHT.*

1. As a supervisor in a bureau, you have been asked by the head of the bureau to recommend whether or not the work of the bureau requires an increase in the permanent staff of the bureau. 1.____
   Of the following questions, the one whose answer would MOST likely assist you in making your recommendation is: Are
   A. some permanent employees working irregular hours because they occasionally work overtime?
   B. the present permanent employees satisfied with their work assignment?
   C. temporary employees hired to handle seasonal fluctuations in work load?
   D. the present permanent employees keeping the work of the bureau current?

2. In making job assignments to his subordinates, a supervisor should follow the principle that each individual GENERALLY is capable of 2.____
   A. performing one type of work well and less capable of performing other types well
   B. learning to perform a wide variety of different types of work
   C. performing best the type of work in which he has had experience
   D. learning to perform any type of work in which he is given training

3. Assume that you are the supervisor of a large number of clerks in a unit in a city agency. Your unit has just been given an important assignment which must be completed a week from now. You know that, henceforth, your unit will be given this assignment every six months. 3.____
   You or any one of your subordinates who has been properly instructed can complete this assignment in one day. This assignment is of a routine type which is ordinarily handled by clerks. There is enough time for you to train one of your subordinates to handle the assignment and then have him do it. However, it would take twice as much time for you to take this course of action as it would for you to do the assignment yourself.
   The one of the following courses of action which you should take in this situation is to
   A. do the assignment yourself as soon as possible without discussing it with any of your subordinates at this time
   B. do the assignment yourself and then train one of your subordinates to handle it in the future
   C. give the assignment to one of your subordinates after training him to handle it
   D. train each of your subordinates to do the assignment on a rotating basis after you have done it yourself the first time

4. You are in charge of an office in which each member of the staff has a different set of duties, although each has the same title. No member of the staff can perform the duties of any other member of the staff without first receiving extensive training. Assume that it is necessary for one member of the staff to take on, in addition to his regular work, an assignment which any member of the staff is capable of carrying out. 4.____
The one of the following considerations which would have the MOST weight in determining which staff member is to be given the additional assignment is the
   A. quality of the work performed by the individual members of the staff
   B. time consumed by individual members of the staff in performing their work
   C. level of difficulty of the duties being performed by individual members of the staff
   D. relative importance of the duties being performed by individual members of the staff

5. The one of the following causes of clerical error which is usually considered to be LEAST attributable to faulty supervision or inefficient management is 5.____
   A. inability to carry out instructions
   B. too much work to do
   C. an inappropriate recordkeeping system
   D. continual interruptions

6. Suppose you are in charge of a large unit in which all of the clerical staff perform similar tasks. 6.____
In evaluating the relative accuracy of the clerks, the clerk who should be considered to be the LEAST accurate is the one
   A. whose errors result in the greatest financial loss
   B. whose errors cost the most to locate
   C. who makes the greatest percentage of errors in his work
   D. who makes the greatest number of errors in the unit

7. Assume that under a proposed procedure for handling employee grievances in a public agency, the first step to be taken is for the aggrieved employee to submit his grievance as soon as it arises to a grievance board set up to hear all employee grievances in the agency. The board, which is to consist of representatives of management and of rank and file employees, is to consider the grievance, obtain all necessary pertinent information, and then render a decision on the matter. Thus, the first-line supervisor would not be involved in the settlement of any of his subordinates' grievances except when asked by the board to submit information. 7.____
This proposed procedure would be generally UNDESIRABLE chiefly because the
   A. board may become a bottleneck to delay the prompt disposition of grievances
   B. aggrieved employees and their supervisors have not been first given the opportunity to resolve the grievances themselves

C. employees would be likely to submit imaginary, as well as real, grievances to the board
D. board will lack first-hand, personal knowledge of the factors involved in grievances

8. Sometimes jobs in private organizations and public agencies are broken down so as to permit a high degree of job specialization. 8.____
Of the following, an IMPORTANT effect of a high degree of job specialization in a public agency is that employees performing
A. highly specialized jobs may not be readily transferable to other jobs in the agency
B. similar duties may require closer supervision than employees performing unrelated functions
C. specialized duties can be held responsible for their work to a greater extent than can employees performing a wide variety of functions
D. specialized duties will tend to cooperate readily with employees performing other types of specialized duties

9. Assume that you are the supervisor of a clerical unit in an agency. One of your subordinates violates a rule of the agency, a violation which requires that the employee be suspended from his work for one day. The violated rule is one that you have found to be unduly strict, and you have recommended to the management of agency that the rule be changed or abolished. The management has been considering your recommendation but has not yet reached a decision on the matter. 9.____
In these circumstances, you should
A. not initiate disciplinary action but, instead, explain to the employee that the rule may be changed shortly
B. delay disciplinary action on the violation until the management has reached a decision on changing the rule
C. modify the disciplinary action by reprimanding the employee and informing him that further action may be taken when the management has reached a decision on changing the rule
D. initiate the prescribed disciplinary action with commenting on the strictness of the rule or on your recommendation

10. Assume that a supervisor praises his subordinates for satisfactory aspects of their work only when he is about to criticize them for unsatisfactory aspects of their work. 10.____
Such a practice is UNDESIRABLE primarily because
A. his subordinates may expect to be praised for their work even if it is unsatisfactory
B. praising his subordinates for some aspects of their work while criticizing other aspects will weaken the effects of the criticisms
C. his subordinates would be more receptive to criticism if it were followed by praise
D. his subordinates may come to disregard praise and wait for criticism to be given

11. The one of the following which would be the BEST reason for an agency to eliminate a procedure for obtaining and recording certain information is that 11.____
    A. it is no longer legally required to obtain the information
    B. there is no advantage in obtaining the information
    C. the information could be compiled on the basis of other information available
    D. the information obtained is sometimes incorrect

12. In determining the type and number of records to be kept in an agency, it is important to recognize that records are of value PRIMARILY as 12.____
    A. raw material to be used in statistical analysis
    B. sources of information about the agency's activities
    C. by-products of the activities carried on by the agency
    D. data for evaluating the effectiveness of the agency

13. Aside from requirements imposed by authority, the frequency with which reports are submitted or the length of the interval which they cover should depend PRINCIPALLY on the 13.____
    A. availability of the data to be included in the reports
    B. amount of time required to prepare the reports
    C. extent of the variations in the data with the passage of time
    D. degree of comprehensiveness required in the reports

14. Organizations that occupy large, general, open-area offices sometimes consider it desirable to build private offices for the supervisors of large bureaus. The one of the following which is generally NOT considered to be a justification of the use of private office is that they 14.____
    A. lend prestige to the person occupying the office
    B. provide facilities for private conferences
    C. achieve the maximum use of office space
    D. provide facilities for performing work requiring a high degree of concentration

15. The LEAST important factor to be considered in planning the layout of an office is the 15.____
    A. relative importance of the different types of work to be done
    B. convenience with which communication can be achieved
    C. functional relationships of the activities of the office
    D. necessity for screening confidential activities from unauthorized persons

16. The one of the following which is generally considered to be the CHIEF advantage of using data processing equipment in modern offices is to 16.____
    A. facilitate the use of a wide variety of sources of information
    B. supply management with current information quickly
    C. provide uniformity in the processing and reporting of information
    D. broaden the area in which management decisions can be made

17. In the box design of office forms, the spaces in which information is to be entered are arranged in boxes containing captions. 17.____
Of the following, the one which is generally NOT considered to be an acceptable rule in employing box design is that
   A. space should be allowed for the lengthiest anticipated entry in a box
   B. the caption should be located in the upper left corner of the box
   C. the boxes on a form should be of the same size and shape
   D. boxes should be aligned vertically whenever possible

18. As a management tool, the work count would generally be of LEAST assistance to a unit supervisor in 18.____
   A. scheduling the work of his unit
   B. locating bottlenecks in the work of his unit
   C. ascertaining the number of subordinates he needs
   D. tracing the flow of work in the unit

19. Of the following, the FIRST step that should be taken in a forms simplification program is to make a 19.____
   A. detailed analysis of the items found on current forms
   B. study of the amount of use made of existing forms
   C. survey of the amount of each kid of form on hand
   D. survey of the characteristics of the more effective forms in use

20. The work-distribution chart is a valuable tool for an office supervisor to use in conducting work simplification programs. 20.____
Of the following questions, the one which a work-distribution chart would generally be LEAST useful in answering is:
   A. What activities take the most time?
   B. Are the employees doing many unrelated tasks?
   C. Is work being distributed evenly among the employees?
   D. Are activities being performed in proper sequence?

21. Assume that, as a supervisor, you conduct, from time to time, work-performance studies in various sections of your agency. The units of measurement used in any study depend on the particular study and may be number of letters typed, number of papers filed, or other suitable units. 21.____
It is MOST important that the units of measurement to be used in a study conform to the units used in similar past studies when the
   A. units of measurement to be used in the study cannot be defined sharply
   B. units of measurement used in past studies were satisfactory
   C results of the study are to be compared with those of past studies
   D. results of the study are to be used for the same purpose as were those of past studies

22. As it is used in auditing, an internal check is a 22.____
   A. procedure which is designed to guard against fraud
   B. periodic audit by a public accounting firm to verify the accuracy of the internal transactions of an organization

C. document transferring funds from one section to another within an organization
D. practice of checking documents twice before they are transmitted outside an organization

23. Of the following, the one which can LEAST be considered to be a proper function of an accounting system is to 23.____
A. indicate the need to curtail expenditures
B. provide information for future fiscal programs
C. record the expenditure of funds from special appropriations
D. suggest method to expedite the collection of revenues

24. Assume that a new unit is to be established in an agency. The unit is to compile and tabulate data so that it will be of the greatest usefulness to the high-level administrators in the agency in making administrative decisions. 24.____
In planning the organization of this unit, the question that should be answered FIRST is:
A. What interpretations are likely to be made of the data by the high-level administrators in making decisions?
B. At what point in the decision-making process will it be most useful to inject the data?
C. What types of data will be required by high-level administrators in making decisions?
D. What criteria will the high-level administrators use to evaluate the decisions they make?

25. The one of the following which is the CHIEF limitation of the organization chart as it is generally used in business and government is that the chart 25.____
A. engenders within incumbents feelings of rights to positions they occupy
B. reveals only formal authority relationships, omitting the informal ones
C. shows varying degrees of authority even though authority is not subject to such differentiation
D. presents organizational structure as it is rather than what it is supposed to be

26. The degree of decentralization that is effective and economical in an organization tends to vary INVERSELY with the 26.____
A. size of the organization
B. availability of adequate numbers of competent personnel
C. physical dispersion of the organization's activities
D. adequacy of the organization's communications system

27. The one of the following which usually can LEAST be considered to be an advantage of committees as they are generally used in government and business is that they 27.____
A. provide opportunities for reconciling varying points of view
B. promote coordination by the interchange of information among the members of the committee

C. act promptly in situations requiring immediate action
D. use group judgment to resolve questions requiring a wide range of experience

28. Managerial decentralization is defined as the decentralization of decision-making authority. 28.____
The degree of managerial decentralization in an organization varies INVERSELY with the
A. number of decisions made lower down the managerial hierarchy
B. importance of the decisions made lower down the management hierarchy
C. number of major organizational functions affected by decisions made at lower management levels
D. amount of review to which decisions made at lower management levels are subjected

29. Some policy-making commissions are composed of members who are appointed to overlapping terms. 29.____
Of the following, the CHIEF advantage of appointing members to overlapping terms in such commissions is that
A. continuity of policy is promoted
B. the likelihood of compromise policy decisions is reduced
C. responsibility for policy decisions can be fixed upon individual members
D. the likelihood of unanimity of opinion is increased

30. If a certain public agency with a fixed number of employees has a line organizational structure, then the width of the span of supervision is 30.____
A. *inversely* proportional to the length of the chain of command in the organization
B. *directly* proportional to the complexity of tasks performed in the organization
C. *inversely* proportional to the competence of the personnel in the organization
D. *directly* proportional to the number of levels of supervision existing in the organization

31. Mr. Brown is a supervisor in charge of a section of clerical employees in an agency. The section consists of four units, each headed by a unit supervisor. From time to time, he makes tours of his section for the purpose of maintaining contact with the rank and file employees. During these tours, he discusses with these employees their work production, work methods, work problems, and other related topics. The information he obtains in this manner is often incomplete or inaccurate. At meeting with the unit supervisors, he questions them on the information acquired during his tours. The supervisors are often unable to answer the questions immediately because they are based on incomplete or inaccurate information. When the supervisors ask that they be permitted to accompany Mr. Brown on his tours and thus answer his questions on the spot, Mr. Brown refuses, explaining that a rank and file employee might be reluctant to speak freely in the presence of his supervisor. 31.____

This situation may BEST be described as a violation of the principle of organization called

A. span of control
B. delegation of authority
C. specialization of work
D. unity of command

Questions 32-36.

DIRECTIONS: Each of Questions 32 through 36 consists of a statement which contains one word that is incorrectly used because it is not in keeping with the meaning that the quotation is evidently intended to convey. For each of these questions, you are to select the INCORRECTLY used word and substitute for it one of the word lettered A, B, C, or D, which helps BEST to convey the meaning of the statement.

32. There has developed in recent years an increasing awareness of the need to measure the quality of management in all enterprise and to seek the principles that can serve as a basis for this improvement. 32.____

A. growth B. raise C. efficiency D. define

33. It is hardly an exaggeration to deny that the permanence, productivity, and humanity of any industrial system depend upon its ability to utilize the positive and constructive impulses of all who work and upon its ability to arouse and continue interest in the necessary activities. 33.____

A. develop B. efficiency C. state D. inspirational

34. The selection of managers on the basis of technical knowledge alone seems to recognize that the essential characteristic of management is getting things done through others, thereby demanding skills that are essential in coordinating the activities of subordinates. 34.____

A. training
B. fails
C. organization
D. improving

35. Only when it is deliberate and when it is clearly understood what impressions the ease of communication will probably create in the minds of employees and subordinate management, should top management refrain from commenting on a subject that is of general concern. 35.____

A. obvious B. benefit C. doubt D. absence

36. Scientific planning of work requires careful analysis of facts and a precise plan of action for the whims and fancies of executives that often provide only a vague indication of the work to be done. 36.____

A. substitutes
B. development
C. preliminary
D. comprehensive

37. Within any single level of government, as a city or a state, the administrative authority may be concentrated or dispersed. 37.____
Of the following plans of government, the one in which administrative authority would be dispersed the MOST is the ____ plan.
A. mayor
B. mayor-council
C. commission
D. city manager

38. In general, the courts may review a decision of an administrative agency with rule-making powers. However, the courts will usually refuse to review a decision of such an agency if the only question raised concerning the decision is whether or not the 38.____
A. decision contravenes public policy
B. agency has abused the powers conferred upon it
C. decision deals with an issue which is within the jurisdiction of the agency
D. agency has applied the same rules of evidence as are used in the courts

39. A legislature sometimes delegates rule-making powers to the administrators of a public agency. 39.____
Of the following, the CHIEF advantage of such delegation is that
A. the frequency with which the legality of the agency's rules is contested in court will be reduced
B. the agency will have the flexibility to adjust to changing conditions and problems
C. mistakes made by the administrators or the legislature in defining the scope of the agency's program may be easily corrected
D. the legislature will not be required to approve the rules formulated by the agency

40. Some municipalities have delegated the functions of budget preparation and personnel selection to central agencies, thus removing these functions from operating departments. 40.____
Of the following, the MOST important reason by municipalities have delegated these functions to central agencies is that
A. the performance of these functions presents problems that vary from one operating department to another
B. operating departments often lack sufficient funds to perform these functions adequately
C. the performance of these functions by a central agency produces more uniform policies than if these functions are performed by the operating departments
D. central agencies are not controlled as closely as are operating departments and so have greater freedom in formulating new policies and procedures to deal with difficult budget and personnel problems

41. Of the following, the MOST fundamental reason for the use of budgets in governmental administration is that budgets 41.____
    A. minimize seasonal variations in workloads and expenditures of public agencies
    B. facilitate decentralization of functions performed by public agencies
    C. provide advance control on the expenditure of funds
    D. establish valid bases for comparing present governmental activities with corresponding activities in previous periods

42. In some governmental jurisdictions, the chief executive prepares the budget for a fiscal period and presents it to the legislative branch of government for adoption. In other jurisdictions, the legislative branch prepares and adopts the budget. 42.____
    Preparation of the budget by the chief executive rather than by the legislative branch is
    A. *desirable*, primarily because the chief executive is held largely accountable by the public for the results of fiscal operations and should, therefore, be the one to prepare the budget
    B. *undesirable*, primarily because such a separation of the legislative and executive branches leads to the enactment of a budget that does not consider the overall needs of the government
    C. *desirable*, primarily because the preparation of the budget by the chief executive limits legislative review and evaluation of operating programs
    D. *undesirable*, primarily because responsibility for budget preparation should be placed in the branch that must eventually adopt the budget and appropriate the funds for it

43. The one of the following which is generally the FIRST step in the budget-making process of a municipality that has a central budget agency is 43.____
    A. determination of available sources of revenue within the municipality
    B. establishment of tax rates at levels sufficient to achieve a balanced budget in the following fiscal period
    C. evaluation by the central budget agency of the adequacy of the municipality's previous budgets
    D. assembling by the central budget agency of the proposed expenditures of each agency in the municipality for the following fiscal period

44. It is advantageous for a municipality to issue serial bonds rather than sinking fund bonds CHIEFLY because 44.____
    A. an issue of serial bonds usually includes a wider range of maturity dates than does an issue of sinking fund bond
    B. appropriations set aside periodically to retire serial bonds as they fall due are more readily invested in long-term securities at favorable rates of interest than are appropriations earmarked for redemption of sinking fund bonds
    C. serial bond are sold at regular intervals while sinking fund bonds are issued as the need for fund arises
    D. a greater variety of interest rates is usually offered in an issue of serial bonds than in an issue of sinking fund bond

45. Studies conducted by the Regional Plan Association of the 22-county New York Metropolitan Region, comprising New York City and surrounding counties in New York, New Jersey, and Connecticut, have defined Manhattan, Brooklyn, Queens, the Bronx, and Hudson County in New Jersey as the core. Such studies have examined the per capita personal income of the core as a percent of the per capita personal income of the entire Region, and the population of the core as a percent of the total population of the entire Region. These studies support the conclusion that, as a percent of the entire Region, 45.____
   A. both population and per capita personal income in the core were higher in 2020 than in 1990
   B. both population and per capita personal income in the core were lower in 2020 than in 1990
   C. population was higher and per capita personal income was lower in the core in 2020 than in 1990
   D. population was lower and per capita personal income was higher in the core in 2020 than in 1990

KEY (CORRECT ANSWERS)

1.	D	11.	B	21.	C	31.	D	41.	C
2.	B	12.	B	22.	A	32.	B	42.	A
3.	C	13.	C	23.	D	33.	C	43.	D
4.	B	14.	C	24.	C	34.	B	44.	A
5.	A	15.	A	25.	B	35.	D	45.	B
6.	C	16.	B	26.	D	36.	A		
7.	B	17.	C	27.	C	37.	C		
8.	A	18.	D	28.	D	38.	D		
9.	D	19.	B	29.	A	39.	B		
10.	D	20.	D	30.	A	40.	C		

ARITHMETIC COMPUTATION

EXAMINATION SECTION

TEST 1

The following sample questions show types of questions that will be used in the written test. They also show how the answers to the questions are to be recorded. Read the directions for each set of questions, and answer them. Record your answers on the Sample Answer Sheets provided on each page of this section. Then compare your answers with those given in the *CORRECT ANSWERS* to Sample Questions on the same page.

Solve each problem and see which of the suggested answers A, B, C, or D is correct. Darken the space on the Sample Answer Sheet corresponding to the correct answer.
If your answer does not exactly agree with any of the first four suggested answers, darken space E.

<u>ADDITION</u>
Questions 1-5.

1. Add: 129
   958
   787
   <u>436</u>

   A. 3310 B. 2308 C. 2312 D. 2310 E. none of these

2.. Add: 9,497
   6,364
   4,269
   <u>9,785</u>

   A 28,915 B. 29,917 C. 29,915 D. 29,925 E. none of these

3. Add: 67,856
   22,851
   44,238
   <u>97,156</u>

   A. 231,101 B. 211,101 C. 212,101 D. 232,111 E. none of these

4. Add: 23
   468
   7
   9,045
   76
   <u>8</u>

   A. 9,627 B. 9,527 C. 9,617 D. 8,627 E none of these

5. Add: 87,651
43,212
76,543
34,564
91,205
<u>34,566</u>

A. 367,641 B. 367,741 C. 368,741 D. 368,641 E. none of these

KEY (CORRECT ANSWERS)

1. D
2. C
3. E
4. A
5. B

SOLUTIONS TO PROBLEMS

1. 129 + 958 + 787 + 436 = 2310
2. 9497 + 6364 + 4269 + 9785 = 29,915
3. 67,856 + 22,851 + 44,238 + 97,156 = 232,141
4. 23 + 468 + 7 + 9045 + 76 +8 = 9627
5. 87,651 + 43,212 + 76,543 + 34,564 + 91,205 + 34,566 = 367,741

TEST 2

SUBTRACTION
Question 1-5.

1. Subtract: 390
   -169

   A. 217 B. 218 C. 219 D. 220 E. none of these

2. Subtract: 639
   -378

   A. 263 B. 262 C. 261 D. 260 E. none of these

3. Subtract: 709
   - 594

   A. 115 B. 114 C. 113 D. 112 E. none of these

4. Subtract: 3,457
   -2,498

   A. 955 B. 956 C. 957 D. 958 E. none of these

5. Subtract: 8,752
   -4,658

   A. 4074 B. 4084 C. 4194 D. 4094 E. none of these

KEY (CORRECT ANSWERS)

1. E
2. C
3. A
4. E
5. D

SOLUTIONS TO PROBLEMS

1. 390 - 169 = 221
2. 639 - 378 = 261
3. 709 - 594 = 115
4. 3457 - 2498 = 959
5. 8752 - 4658 = 4094

TEST 3

MULTIPLICATION
Questions 1-5.

1. Multiply: 36
   x5

   A. 190   B. 160   C.180   D. 365   E. none of these

2. Multiply: 86
   x6

   A. 486   B. 506   C. 536   D. 866   E. none of these

3. Multiply: 40
   x4

   A. 160   B. 440   C. 164   D. 180   E. none of these

4. Multiply: 95
   x2

   A. 952   B. 180   C. 190   D. 195   E. none of these

5. Multiply: 52
   x7

   A. 347   B. 346   C. 527   D. 364   E. none of these

KEY (CORRECT ANSWERS)

1. C
2. E
3. A
4. C
5. D

SOLUTIONS TO PROBLEMS

1. (36)(5) = 180
2. (86)(6) = 516
3. (40)(4) = 160
4. (95)(2) = 190
5. (52)(7) = 364

TEST 4

DIVISION
Questions 1-5.

1. Divide: 546÷9

   A. 60 B. 60 3/9 C. 60 6/9 D. 61 E. none of these

2. Divide: $8\overline{)247}$

   A. 30 B. 30 1/8 C. 30 3/8 D. 30 5/8 E. none of these

3. Divide: $\frac{289}{4}$

   A. 72 B. 72 1/8 C. 72 3/8 D. 72 ½ E. none of these

4. Divide: 363÷4

   A. 91 B. 92 C. 90 ¼ D. 90 ¾ E. none of these

5. Divide: $\frac{304}{4}$

   A. 75 1/4 B. 76 C. 75 ¼ D. 76 ¼ E. none of these

KEY (CORRECT ANSWERS)

1. C
2. E
3. E
4. D
5. B

SOLUTIONS TO PROBLEMS

1. 546 ÷ 9 = 60 6/9 or 60 2/3
2. 247 ÷ 8 = 30.875 = 30 7/8
3. 289 ÷ 4 = 72.25 = 72 1/4
4. 363 ÷ 4 = 90.75 = 90 3/4
5. 304 ÷ 4 = 76

ARITHMETICAL COMPUTATION AND REASONING
EXAMINATION SECTION
TEST 1

DIRECTIONS: Each question or incomplete statement is followed by several suggested answers or completions. Select the one that BEST answers the question or completes the statement. *PRINT THE LETTER OF THE CORRECT ANSWER IN THE SPACE AT THE RIGHT.*

1. 3/8 less than $40 is 1.____

   A. $25 B. $65 C. $15 D. $55

2. 27/64 expressed as a percent is 2.____

   A. 40.625% B. 42.188% C. 43.750% D. 45.313%

3. 1/6 more than 36 gross is ______ gross. 3.____

   A. 6 B. 48 C. 30 D. 42

4. 15 is 20% of 4.____

5. The number which when increased by 1/3 of itself equals 96 is 5.____

   A. 128 B. 72 C. 64 D. 32

6. 0.16 3/4 written as percent is 6.____

   A. 16 3/4% B. 16.3/4% C. .016 3/4% D. .0016 3/4%

7. 55% of 15 is 7.____

   A. 82.5 B. 0.825 C. 0.0825 D. 8.25

8. The number which when decreased by 1/3 of itself equals 96 is 8.____

   A. 64 B. 32 C. 128 D. 144

9. A carpenter used a board 15 3/4 ft. long from which 3 footstools were made with sufficient lumber left over for half of another footstool.
   If the lumber cost 24 1/2¢ per foot, the cost of EACH footstool was 9.____

   A. $1.54 B. $3.86 C. $1.10 D. $1.08

10. In one year, a luncheonette purchased 1231 gallons of milk for $907.99.
    The AVERAGE cost per half pint was 10.____

    A. $0.046 B. $0.045 C. $0.047 D. $0.044

11. The product of 23 and 9 3/4 is 11.____

    A. 191 2/3 B. 224 1/4 C. 213 3/4 D. 32 3/4

12. An order for 345 machine bolts at $4.15 per hundred will cost 12.____

    A. $0.1432 B. $1.1432 C. $14.32 D. $143.20

13. The fractional equivalent of .0625 is 13.____

A. 1/16 B. 1/15 C. 1/14 D. 1/13

14. The number 0.03125 equals 14.____

A. 3/64 B. 1/16 C. 1/64 D. 1/32

15. 21.70 divided by 1.75 equals 15.____

A. 124 B. 12.4 C. 1.24 D. .124

16. The average cost of school lunches for 100 children varied as follows: Monday, $0.285; Tuesday, $0.237; Wednesday, $0.264; Thursday, $0.276; Friday, $0.292. The AVERAGE lunch cost 16.____

A. $0.136 B. $0.270 C. $0.135 D. $0.271

17. The cost of 5 dozen eggs at $8.52 per gross is 17.____

A. $3.50 B. $42.60 C. $3.55 D. $3.74

18. 410.07 less 38.49 equals 18.____

A. 372.58 B. 371.58 C. 381.58 D. 382.68

19. The cost of 7 3/4 tons of coal at $20.16 per ton is 19.____

A. $15.12 B. $151.20 C. $141.12 D. $156.24

20. The sum of 90.79, 79.09, 97.90, and 9.97 is 20.____

A. 277.75 B. 278.56 C. 276.94 D. 277.93

KEY (CORRECT ANSWERS)

1. A	11. B
2. B	12. C
3. D	13. A
4. C	14. D
5. B	15. B
6. A	16. D
7. D	17. C
8. D	18. B
9. C	19. D
10. A	20. A

SOLUTIONS TO PROBLEMS

1. ($40)(5/8) = $25

2. 27/64 = .421875 ≈ 42.188%

3. (36)(1 1/6) = 42

4. Let x = missing number. Then, 15 = .20x. Solving, x = 75

5. Let x = missing number. Then, x + 1/3 x = 96. Simplifying, 4/3 x = 96. Solving, x = 96 ÷ 4/3 = 72

6. .16 3/4 = 16 3/4% by simply moving the decimal point two places to the right.

7. (.55)(15) = 8.25

8. Let x = missing number. Then, x - 1/3 x = 96. Simplifying, 2/3 x = 96. Solving, x = 96 ÷ 2/3 = 144

9. 15 3/4 ÷ 3 1/2 = 4.5 feet per footstool. The cost of one footstool is ($.245)(4.5) = $1.1025 ≈ $1.10

10. $907.99 ÷ 1231 = $.7376 per gallon. Since there are 16 half-pints in a gallon, the average cost per half-pint is $.7376 ÷ 16 ≈ $.046

11. (23)(9 3/4) = (23)(9.75) = 224.25 or 224 1/4

12. ($4.15)(3.45) = $14.3175 = $14.32

13. .0625 = 625/10,000 = 1/16

14. .03125 = 3125/100,000 = 1/32

15. 21.70 ÷ 1.75 = 12.4

16. The sum of these lunches is $1.354. Then, $1.354 ÷ 5 = $.2708 = $.271

17. $8.52 ÷ 12 = $.71 per dozen. Then, the cost of 5 dozen is ($.71)(5) = $3.55

18. 410.07 - 38.49 = 371.58

19. ($20.16)(7.75) = $156.24

20. 90.79 + 79.09 + 97.90 + 9.97 = 277.75

TEST 2

DIRECTIONS: Each question or incomplete statement is followed by several suggested answers or completions. Select the one that BEST answers the question or completes the statement. *PRINT THE LETTER OF THE CORRECT ANSWER IN THE SPACE AT THE RIGHT.*

1. 1600 is 40% of what number? 1.____

   A. 6400 B. 3200 C. 4000 D. 5600

2. An executive's time card reads: Arrived 9:15 A.M., Left 2:05 P.M. How many hours was he in the office? _______ hours _______ minutes. 2.____

   A. 5; 10 B. 4; 50 C. 4; 10 D. 5; 50

3. .4266 times .3333 will have the following number of decimals in the product: 3.____

   A. 8 B. 4 C. 1 D. None of these

4. An office floor is 25 ft. wide by 36 ft. long. To cover this floor with carpet will require _______ square yards. 4.____

   A. 100 B. 300 C. 900 D. 25

5. 1/8 of 1% expressed as a decimal is 5.____

   A. .125 B. .0125 C. 1.25 D. .00125

6. $\frac{6 \div 4}{6 \times 4}$ equals 6x4 6.____

   A. 1/16 B. 1 C. 1/6 D. 1/4

7. 1/25 of 230 equals 7.____

   A. 92.0 B. 9.20 C. .920 D. 920

8. 4 times 3/8 equals 8.____

   A. 1 3/8 B. 3/32 C. 12.125 D. 1.5

9. 3/4 divided by 4 equals 9.____

   A. 3 B. 3/16 C. 16/3 D. 16

10. 6/7 divided by 2/7 equals 10.____

   A. 6 B. 12/49 C. 3 D. 21

11. The interest on $240 for 90 days ' 6% is 11.____

   A. $4.80 B. $3.40 C. $4.20 D. $3.60

12. 16 2/3% of 1728 is 12.____

   A. 91 B. 288 C. 282 D. 280

13. 6 1/4% of 6400 is 13.____

A. 2500 B. 410 C. 108 D. 400

14. 12 1/2% of 560 is 14.____

A. 65 B. 40 C. 50 D. 70

15. 2 yards divided by 3 equals 15.____

A. 2 feet B. 1/2 yard C. 3 yards D. 3 feet

16. A school has 540 pupils. 45% are boys. How many girls are there in this school? 16.____

A. 243 B. 297 C. 493 D. 394

17. .1875 is equivalent to 17.____

A. 18 3/4 B. 75/18 C. 18/75 D. 3/16

18. A kitchen cabinet listed at $42 is sold for $33.60. The discount allowed is 18.____

A. 10% B. 15% C. 20% D. 30%

19. 3 6/8 divided by 8 1/4 equals 19.____

A. 9 1/8 B. 12 C. 5/11 D. 243.16

20. An agent sold goods to the amount of $1480. His commission at 5 1/2% was 20.____

A. $37.50 B. $81.40 C. 76.70 D. $81.10

KEY (CORRECT ANSWERS

1.	C	11.	D
2.	B	12.	B
3.	A	13.	D
4.	A	14.	D
5.	D	15.	A
6.	A	16.	B
7.	B	17.	D
8.	D	18.	C
9.	B	19.	C
10.	C	20.	B

SOLUTIONS TO PROBLEMS

1. Let x = missing number. Then, 1600 = .40x. Solving, x = 4000
2. 2:05 PM - 9:15 AM = 4 hours 50 minutes
3. The product of two 4-decimal numbers is an 8-decimal number.
4. (25 ft)(36 ft) = 900 sq.ft. = 100 sq.yds.
5. (1/8)(1%) = (.125)(.01) = .00125
6. (6 ÷ 4) ÷ (6 x 4) = 3/2 ÷ 24 = (3/2)(1/24)= (1/16)
7. (1/25)(230) = 9.20
8. (4)(3/8) = 12/8 = 1.5
9. 3/4 ÷ 4 = (3/4)(1/4) = 3/16
10. 6/7 / 2/7 = (6/7)(7/2) = 3
11. ($240)(.06)(90/360) = $3.60
12. (16 2/3%)(1728) = (1/6)(1728) = 288
13. (6 1/4%)(6400) = (1/16)(6400) = 400
14. (12 1/2%)(560) = (1/8)(560) = 70
15. 2 yds ÷ 3 = 2/3 yds = (2/3)(3) = 2 ft.
16. If 45% are boys, then 55% are girls. Thus, (540)(.55) = 297
17. .1875 = 1875/10,000 = 3/16
18. $42 - $33.60 = $8.40.
    The discount is $8.40 ÷ $42 = .20 = 20%
19. 3 6/8 - 8 1/4 = (30/8)(4/33) = 5/11
20. ($1480)(.055) = $81.40

TEST 3

DIRECTIONS: Each question or incomplete statement is followed by several suggested answers or completions. Select the one that BEST answers the question or completes the statement. *PRINT THE LETTER OF THE CORRECT ANSWER IN THE SPACE AT THE RIGHT.*

1. 93.648 divided by 0.4 is 1.____

   A. 23.412 B. 234.12 C. 2.3412 D. 2341.2

2. Add 4.3682, .0028, 34., 9.92, and from the sum subtract 1.992. The remainder is 2.____

   A. .46299 B. 4.6299 C. 462.99 D. 46.299

3. At $2.88 per gross, three dozen will cost 3.____

   A. $8.64 B. $0.96 C. $0.72 D. $11.52

4. 13 times 2.39 times 0.024 equals 4.____

   A. 745.68 B. 74.568 C. 7.4568 D. .74568

5. A living room suite is marked $64 less 25 percent. A cash discount of 10 percent is allowed. The cash price is 5.____

   A. $53.20 B. $47.80 C. $36.00 D. $43.20

6. 1/8 of 1 percent expressed as a decimal is 6.____

   A. .125 B. .0125 C. 1.25 D. .00125

7. 16 percent of 482.11 equals 7.____

   A. 77.1376 B. 771.4240 C. 7714.2400 D. 7.71424

8. A merchant sold a chair for $60. This was at a profit of 25 percent of what it cost him. The chair cost him 8.____

   A. $48 B. $45 C. $15 D. $75

9. Add 5 hours 13 minutes, 3 hours 49 minutes, and 14 minutes. The sum is ______ hours ______ minutes. 9.____

   A. 9; 16 B. 9;76 C. 8;16 D. 8;6

10. 89 percent of $482 is 10.____

    A. $428.98 B. $472.36 C. $42.90 D. $47.24

11. 200 percent of 800 is 11.____

    A. 16 B. 1600 C. 2500 D. 4

12. Add 2 feet 3 inches, 4 feet 11 inches, 8 inches, 6 feet 6 inches. The sum is ______ feet ______ inches. 12.____

    A. 12; 4 B. 12; 14 C. 14; 4 D. 14; 28

13. A merchant bought dresses at $15 each and sold them at $20 each. His overhead expenses are 20 percent of cost. His net profit on each dress is 13.____

A. $1 B. $2 C. $3 D. $4

14. 0.0325 expressed as a percent is 14.____

A. 325% B. 3 1/4% C. 32 1/2% D. 32.5%

15. Add 3/4, 1/8, 1/32, 1/2; and from the sum subtract 4/8. The remainder is 15.____

A. 2/32 B. 7/8 C. 29/32 D. 3/4

16. A salesman gets a commission of 4 percent on his sales. If he wants his commission to amount to $40, he will have to sell merchandise totaling 16.____

A. $160 B. $10 C. $1,000 D. $100

17. Jones borrowed $225,000 for five years at 3 1/2 percent. The annual interest charge was 17.____

A. $1,575 B. $1,555 C. $7,875 D. $39,375

18. A kitchen cabinet listed at $42 is sold for $33.60. The discount allowed is ______ percent. 18.____

A. 10 B. 15 C. 20 D. 30

19. The exact number of days from May 5, 2007 to July 1, 2007 is ______ days. 19.____

A. 59 B. 58 C. 56 D. 57

20. A dealer sells an article at a loss of 50% of the cost. Based on the selling price, the loss is 20.____

A. 25% B. 50% C. 100% D. none of these

KEY (CORRECT ANSWERS)

1. B
2. D
3. C
4. D
5. D

6. D
7. A
8. A
9. A
10. A

11. B
12. C
13. B
14. B
15. C

16. C
17. C
18. C
19. D
20. C

SOLUTIONS TO PROBLEMS

1. 93.648 ÷ .4 = 234.12
2. 4.368 + .0028 + 34 + 9.92 - 1.992 = 48.291 - 1.992 = 46.299
3. $2.88 for 12 dozen means $.24 per dozen. Three dozen will cost (3)($.24) = $.72
4. (13)(2.39)(.024) = .74568
5. ($64)(.75)(.90) = $43.20
6. (1/8)(1%) = (.125)(.01) = .00125
7. (.16)(482.11) = 77.1376
8. Let x = cost. Then, 1.25x = $60. Solving, x = $48
9. 5 hrs. 13 min. + 3 hrs. 49 min. + 14 min = 8 hrs. 76 min.
10. (.89)($482) = $428.98
11. 200% = 2. So, (200%)(800) = (2)(800) = 1600
12. 2 ft. 3 in. + 4 ft. 11 in. + 8 in. + 6 ft. 6 in. + 12 ft. 28 in. = 14 ft. 4 in.
13. Overhead is (.20)($15) = $3. The net profit is $20 - $15 - $3 = $2
14. .0325 = 3.25% = 3 1/4%
15. 3/4 + 1/8 + 1/32 + 1/2 - 4/8 = 45/32 - 4/8 = 29/32
16. Let x = sales. Then, $40 = .04x. Solving, x = $1000
17. Annual interest is ($225,000)(.035) x 1 = 7875
18. $42 - $33.60 = $8.40. Then, $8.40 ÷ $42 = .20 = 20%
19. The number of days left for May, June, July is 26, 30, and 1. Thus, 26 + 30 + 1 = 57
20. Let x = cost, so that .50x = selling price. The loss is represented by .50x ÷ .50x = 1 = 100% on the selling price. (Note: The loss in dollars is x - .50x = .50x)

CLERICAL ABILITIES TEST

EXAMINATION SECTION

TEST 1

DIRECTIONS: Each question or incomplete statement is followed by several suggested answers or completions. Select the one that BEST answers the question or completes the statement. *PRINT THE LETTER OF THE CORRECT ANSWER IN THE SPACE AT THE RIGHT.*

Questions 1-10.

DIRECTIONS: Questions 1 through 10 consist of lines of names, dates, and numbers. For each question, you are to choose the option (A, B, C, or D) in Column II which EXACTLY matches the information in Column I. *PRINT THE LETTER OF THE CORRECT ANSWER IN THE SPACE AT THE RIGHT.*

SAMPLE QUESTION

Column I	Column II
Schneider 11/16/75 581932	A. Schneider 11/16/75 518932
	B. Schneider 11/16/75 581932
	C. Schnieder 11/16/75 581932
	D. Shnieder 11/16/75 518932

The correct answer is B. Only Option B shows the name, date, and number exactly as they are in Column I. Option A has a mistake in the number. Option C has a mistake in the name. Option D has a mistake in the name and in the number. Now answer Questions 1 through 10 in the same manner.

	Column I	Column II	
1.	Johnston 12/26/74 659251	A. Johnson 12/23/74 659251	1.____
		B. Johston 12/26/74 659251	
		C. Johnston 12/26/74 695251	
		D. Johnston 12/26/74 659251	
2.	Allison 1/26/75 9939256	A. Allison 1/26/75 9939256	2.____
		B. Alisson 1/26/75 9939256	
		C. Allison 1/26/76 9399256	
		D. Allison 1/26/75 9993356	
3.	Farrell 2/12/75 361251	A. Farell 2/21/75 361251	3.____
		B. Farrell 2/12/75 361251	
		C. Farrell 2/21/75 361251	
		D. Farrell 2/12/75 361151	

4. Guerrero 4/28/72 105689
A. Guererro 4/28/72 105689
B. Guererro 4/28/72 105986
C. Guerrero 4/28/72 105869
D. Guerrero 4/28/72 105689
4.____

5. McDonnell 6/05/73 478215
A. McDonnell 6/15/73 478215
B. McDonnell 6/05/73 478215
C. McDonnell 6/05/73 472815
D. MacDonell 6/05/73 478215
5.____

6. Shepard 3/31/71 075421
A. Sheperd 3/31/71 075421
B. Shepard 3/13/71 075421
C. Shepard 3/31/71 075421
D. Shepard 3/13/71 075241
6.____

7. Russell 4/01/69 031429
A. Russell 4/01/69 031429
B. Russell 4/10/69 034129
C. Russell 4/10/69 031429
D. Russell 4/01/69 034129
7.____

8. Phillips 10/16/68 961042
A. Philipps 10/16/68 961042
B. Phillips 10/16/68 960142
C. Phillips 10/16/68 961042
D. Philipps 10/16/68 916042
8.____

9. Campbell 11/21/72 624856
A. Campbell 11/21/72 624856
B. Campbell 11/21/72 624586
C. Campbell 11/21/72 624686
D. Campbel 11/21/72 624856
9.____

10. Patterson 9/18/71 76199176
A. Patterson 9/18/72 76191976
B. Patterson 9/18/71 76199176
C. Patterson 9/18/72 76199176
D. Patterson 9/18/71 76919176
10.____

Questions 11-15.

DIRECTIONS: Questions 11 through 15 consist of groups of numbers and letters which you are to compare. For each question, you are to choose the option (A, B,C, or D) in Column I which EXACTLY matches the group of numbers and letters given in Column I.

SAMPLE QUESTION

Column I	Column II
B92466	A. B92644
	B. B94266
	C. A92466
	D. B92466

The correct answer is D. Only Option D in Column II shows the group of numbers and letters EXACTLY as it appears in Column I. Now answer Questions 11 through 15 in the same manner.

	Column I	Column II	
11.	925AC5	A. 952CA5 B. 925AC5 C. 952AC5 D. 925CA6	11.____
12.	Y006925	A. Y060925 B. Y006295 C. Y006529 D. Y006925	12.____
13.	J236956	A. J236956 B. J326965 C. J239656 D. J932656	13.____
14.	AB6952	A. AB6952 B. AB9625 C. AB9652 D. AB6925	14.____
15.	X259361	A. X529361 B. X259631 C. X523961 D. X259361	15.____

Questions 16-25.

DIRECTIONS: Each of questions 16 through 25 consists of three lines of code letters and three lines of numbers. The numbers on each line should correspond with the code letters on the same line in accordance with the table below.

Code Letter	S	V	W	A	Q	M	X	E	G	K
Corresponding Number	0	1	2	3	4	5	5	7	8	9

On some of the lines, an error exists in the coding. Compare the letters and numbers in each question carefully. If you find an error or errors on:

only one of the lines in the question, mark your answer A;
any two lines in the question, mark your answer B;
all three lines in the question, mark your answer C;
none of the lines in the question, mark your answer D.

SAMPLE QUESTION

WQGKSXG	2489068
XEKVQMA	6591453
KMAESXV	9527061

In the above sample, the first line is correct since each code letter listed has the correct corresponding number. On the second line, an error exists because code letter E should have the number 7 instead of the number 5. On the third line, an error exists because the code letter A should have the number 3 instead of the number 2. Since there are errors in two of the three lines, the correct answer is B. Now answer Questions 16 through 25 in the same manner.

16.	SWQEKGA	0247983	16.____
	KEAVSXM	9731065	
	SSAXGKQ	0036894	
17.	QAMKMVS	4259510	17.____
	MGGEASX	5897306	
	KSWMKWS	9125920	
18.	WKXQWVE	2964217	18.____
	QKXXQVA	4966413	
	AWMXGVS	3253810	
19.	GMMKASE	8559307	19.____
	AWVSKSW	3210902	
	QAVSVGK	4310189	
20.	XGKQSMK	6894049	20.____
	QSVKEAS	4019730	
	GSMXKMV	8057951	
21.	AEKMWSG	3195208	21.____
	MKQSVQK	5940149	
	XGQAEVW	6843712	
22.	XGMKAVS	6858310	22.____
	SKMAWEQ	0953174	
	GVMEQSA	8167403	
23.	VQSKAVE	1489317	23.____
	WQGKAEM	2489375	
	MEGKAWQ	5689324	
24.	XMQVSKG	6541098	24.____
	QMEKEWS	4579720	
	KMEVGKG	9571983	

25. GKVAMEW 88912572 25.____
AXMVKAE 3651937
KWAGMAV 9238531

Questions 26-35.

DIRECTIONS: Each of Questions 26 through 35 consists of a column of figures. For each question, add the column of figures and choose the correct answer from the four choices given.

26. 26.____
5,665.43
2,356.69
6,447.24
7,239.65

A. 20,698.01
B. 21,709.01
C. 21,718.01
D. 22,609.01

27. 27.____
817,209.55
264,354.29
82,368.76
849,964.89

A. 1,893.977.49
B. 1,989,988.39
C. 2,009,077.39
D. 2,013,897.49

28. 28.____
156,366.89
249,973.23
823,229.49
56,869.45

A. 1,286,439.06
B. 1,287,521.06
C. 1,297,539.06
D. 1,296,421.06

29. 29.____
23,422.15
149,696.24
238,377.53
86,289.79
505,533.63

A. 989,229.34
B. 999,879.34
C. 1,003,330.34
D. 1,023,329.34

30. 2,468,926.70 30.____
656,842.28
49,723.15
832,369.59

A. 3,218,062.72
B. 3,808,092.72
C. 4,007,861.72
D. 4,818,192.72

31. 524,201.52 31.____
7,775,678.51
8,345,299.63
40,628,898.08
31,374,670.07

A. 88,646,647.81
B. 88,646,747.91
C. 88,648,647.91
D. 88,648,747.81

32. 6,824,829.40 32.____
682,482.94
5,542,015.27
775,678.51
7,732,507.25

A. 21,557,513.37
B. 21,567,513.37
C. 22,567,503.37
D. 22,567,513.37

33. 22,109,405.58 33.____
6,097,093.43
5,050,073.99
8,118,050.05
4,313,980.82

A. 45,688,593.87
B. 45,688,603.87
C. 45,689,593.87
D. 45,689,603.87

34. 79,324,114.19 34.____
99,848,129.74
43,331,653.31
41,610,207.14

A. 264,114,104.38
B. 264,114,114.38
C. 265,114,114.38
D. 265,214,104.38

35. 33,729,653.94 35.____
 5,959,342.58
26,052,715.47
 4,452,669.52
 7,079,953.59

A. 76,374,334.10
B. 76,375,334.10
C. 77,274,335.10
D. 77,275,335.10

Questions 36-40.

DIRECTIONS: Each of Questions 36 through 40 consists of a single number in Column I and four options in Column II. For each question, you are to choose the option (A, B, C, or D) in Column II which EXACTLY matches the number in Column I.

SAMPLE QUESTION

Column I	Column II
5965121	A. 5956121
	B. 5965121
	C. 5966121
	D. 5965211

The correct answer is B. Only Option B shows the number EXACTLY as it appears in Column I. Now answer Questions 36 through 40 in the same manner.

	Column I	Column II	
36.	9643242	A. 9643242	36.____
		B. 9462342	
		C. 9642442	
		D. 9463242	
37.	3572477	A. 3752477	37.____
		B. 3725477	
		C. 3572477	
		D. 3574277	
38.	5276101	A. 5267101	38.____
		B. 5726011	
		C. 5271601	
		D. 5276101	
39.	4469329	A. 4496329	39.____
		B. 4469329	
		C. 4496239	
		D. 4469239	

40. 2326308

A. 2236308
B. 2233608
C. 2326308
D. 2323608

40.____

KEY (CORRECT ANSWERS)

1.	D	11.	B	21.	A	31.	D
2.	A	12.	D	22.	C	32.	A
3.	B	13.	A	23.	B	33.	B
4.	D	14.	A	24.	D	34.	A
5.	B	15.	D	25.	A	35.	C
6.	C	16.	D	26.	B	36.	A
7.	A	17.	C	27.	D	37.	C
8.	C	18.	A	28.	A	38.	D
9.	A	19.	D	29.	C	39.	B
10.	B	20.	B	30.	C	40.	C

TEST 2

DIRECTIONS: Each question or incomplete statement is followed by several suggested answers or completions. Select the one that BEST answers the question or completes the statement. *PRINT THE LETTER OF THE CORRECT ANSWER IN THE SPACE AT THE RIGHT.*

Questions 1-5.

DIRECTIONS: Each of Questions 1 through 5 consists of a name and a dollar amount. In each question, the name and dollar amount in Column II should be an EXACT copy of the name and dollar amount in Column I. If there is:
a mistake only in the name, mark your answer A;
a mistake only in the dollar amount, mark your answer B;
a mistake in both the name and the dollar amount, mark your answer C;
no mistake in either the name or the dollar amount, mark your answer D.

SAMPLE QUESTION

Column I	Column II
George Peterson $125.50	George Petersson $125.50

Compare the name and dollar amount in Column II with the name and dollar amount in Column I. The name *Petersson* in Column II is spelled *Peterson* in Column I. The amount is the same in both columns. Since there is a mistake only in the name, the answer to the sample question is A. Now answer Questions 1 through 5 in the same manner.

	Column I	Column II	
1.	Susanne Shultz $3440	Susanne Schultz $3440	1.____
2.	Anibal P. Contrucci $2121.61	Anibel P. Contrucci $2112.61	2.____
3.	Eugenio Mendoza $12.45	Eugenio Mendozza $12.45	3.____
4.	Maurice Gluckstadt $4297	Maurice Gluckstadt $4297	4.____
5.	John Pampellonne $4656.94	John Pammpellonne $4566.94	5.____

Questions 6-11.

DIRECTIONS: Each of Questions 6 through 11 consist of a set of names and addresses, which you are to compare. In each question, the name and addresses in Column II should be an EXACT copy of the name and address in Column I. If there is:
a mistake only in the name, mark your answer A;
a mistake only in the address, mark your answer B;
a mistake in both the name and address, mark your answer C;
no mistake in either the name or address, mark your answer D.

SAMPLE QUESTION

Column I	Column II
Michael Filbert 456 Reade Street New York, N.Y. 10013	Michael Filbert 645 Reade Street New York, N.Y. 10013

Since there is a mistake only in the address (the street number should be 456 instead of 645), the answer to the sample question is B. Now answer Questions 6 through 11 in the same manner.

	Column I	Column II	
6.	Hilda Goettelmann 55 Lenox Rd. Brooklyn, N.Y. 11226	Hilda Goettelman 55 Lenox Ave. Brooklyn, N.Y. 11226	6.____
7.	Arthur Sherman 2522 Batchelder St. Brooklyn, N.Y. 11235	Arthur Sharman 2522 Batcheder St. Brooklyn, N.Y. 11253	7.____
8.	Ralph Barnett 300 West 28 Street New York, New York 10001	Ralph Barnett 300 West 28 Street New York, New York 10001	8.____
9.	George Goodwin 135 Palmer Avenue Staten Island, New York 10302	George Godwin 135 Palmer Avenue Staten Island, New York 10302	9.____
10.	Alonso Ramirez 232 West 79 Street New York, N.Y. 10024	Alonso Ramirez 223 West 79 Street New York, N.Y. 10024	10.____
11.	Cynthia Graham 149-34 83 Street Howard Beach, N.Y. 11414	Cynthia Graham 149-35 83 Street Howard Beach, N.Y. 11414	11.____

Questions 12-20.

DIRECTIONS: Questions 12 through 20 are problems in subtraction. For each question do the subtraction and select your answer from the four choices given.

12. 232,921.85
-179,587.68 12.____

A. 52,433.17 B. 52,434.17
C. 53,334.17 D. 53,343,17

13. 5,531,876.29
-3,897,158.36 13.____

A. 1,634,717.93 B. 1,644,718.93
C. 1,734,717.93 D. 1,7234,718.93

14. 1,482,658.22
-937,925.76 14.____

A. 544,633.46 B. 544,732.46
C. 545,632.46 D. 545,732.46

15. 937,828.17
-259,673.88 15.____

A. 678,154.29 B. 679,154.29
C. 688,155.39 D. 699,155.39

16. 760,412.38
-263,465.95 16.____

A. 496,046.43 B. 496,946.43
C. 496,956.43 D. 497,046.43

17. 3,203,902.26
-2,933,087.96 17.____

A. 260,814.30 B. 269,824.30
C. 270,814.30 D. 270,824.30

18. 1,023,468.71
-934,678.88 18.____

A. 88,780.83 B. 88,789.83
C. 88,880.83 D. 88,889.83

19. 831,549.47 19.____
-772,814.78

A. 58,734.69 B. 58,834.69
C. 59,735.69 D. 59,834.69

20. 6,306,181.74 20.____
-3,617,376.99

A. 2,687,904.99 B. 2,688,904.99
C. 2,689,804.99 D. 2,799,905.99

Questions 21-30.

DIRECTIONS: Each of Questions 21 through 30 consists of three lines of code letters and three lines of numbers. The numbers on each line should correspond with the code letters on the same line in accordance with the table below.

Code Letter	J	U	B	T	Y	D	K	R	L	P
Corresponding Number	0	1	2	3	4	5	5	7	8	9

On some of the lines, an error exists in the coding. Compare the letters and numbers in each question carefully. If you find an error or errors on:
only *one* of the lines in the question, mark your answer A;
any *two* lines in the question, mark your answer B;
all *three* lines in the question, mark your answer C;
none of the lines in the question, mark your answer D.

SAMPLE QUESTION

BJRPYUR 2079417
DTBPYKJ 5328460
YKLDBLT 4685283

In the above sample, the first line is correct since each code letter listed has the correct corresponding number. On the second line, an error exists because code letter P should have the number 9 instead of the number 8. The third line is correct since each code letter listed has the correct corresponding number. Since there is an error in *one* of the three lines, the correct answer is A. Now answer Questions 21 through 30 in the same manner.

21. BYPDTJL 2495308 21.____
PLRDTJU 9815301
DTJRYLK 5207486

22. RPBYRJK 7934706 22.____
PKTYLBU 9624821
KDLPJYR 6489047

23.	TPYBUJR BYRKPTU DUKPYDL	3942107 2476931 5169458	23.____
24.	KBYDLPL BLRKBRU JTULDYB	6345898 2876261 0318542	24.____
25.	LDPYDKR BDKDRJL BDRPLUJ	8594567 2565708 2679810	25.____
26.	PLRLBPU LPYKRDJ TDKPDTR	9858291 88936750 3569527	26.____
27.	RKURPBY RYUKPTJ RTKPTJD	7617924 7426930 7369305	27.____
28.	DYKPBJT KLPJBTL TKPLBJP	5469203 6890238 3698209	28.____
29.	BTPRJYL LDKUTYR YDBLRPJ	2397148 8561347 4528190	29.____
30.	ULPBKYT KPDTRBJ YLKJPTB	1892643 6953720 4860932	30.____

KEY (CORRECT ANSWERS)

1.	A	11.	D	21.	B
2.	C	12.	C	22.	C
3.	A	13.	A	23.	D
4.	D	14.	B	24.	B
5.	C	15.	A	25.	A
6.	C	16.	B	26.	C
7.	C	17.	C	27.	A
8.	D	18.	B	28.	D
9.	A	19.	A	29.	B
10.	B	20.	B	30.	D

RECORD KEEPING
EXAMINATION SECTION
TEST 1

DIRECTIONS: Each question or incomplete statement is followed by several suggested answers or completions. Select the one that BEST answers the question or completes the statement. *PRINT THE LETTER OF THE CORRECT ANSWER IN THE SPACE AT THE RIGHT.*

Questions 1-7.

DIRECTIONS: In answering Questions 1 through 7, use the following master list. For each question, determine where the name would fit on the master list. Each answer choice indicates right before or after the name in the answer choice.

Aaron, Jane
Armstead, Brendan
Bailey, Charles
Dent, Ricardo
Grant, Mark
Mars, Justin
Methieu, Justine
Parker, Cathy
Sampson, Suzy
Thomas, Heather

1. Schmidt, William 1.____
   A. Right before Cathy Parker
   B. Right after Heather Thomas
   C. Right after Suzy Sampson
   D. Right before Ricardo Dent

2. Asanti, Kendall 2.____
   A. Right before Jane Aaron
   B. Right after Charles Bailey
   C. Right before Justine Methieu
   D. Right after Brendan Armstead

3. O'Brien, Daniel 3.____
   A. Right after Justine Methieu
   B. Right before Jane Aaron
   C. Right after Mark Grant
   D. Right before Suzy Sampson

4. Marrow, Alison 4.____
   A. Right before Cathy Parker
   B. Right before Justin Mars
   C. Right before Mark Grant
   D. Right after Heather Thomas

5. Grantt, Marissa 5.____
   A. Right before Mark Grant
   B. Right after Mark Grant
   C. Right after Justin Mars
   D. Right before Suzy Sampson

6. Thompson, Heath 6.____
   A. Right after Justin Mars
   B. Right before Suzy Sampson
   C. Right after Heather Thomas
   D. Right before Cathy Parker

DIRECTIONS: Before answering Question 7, add in all of the names from Questions 1 through 6. Then fit the name in alphabetical order based on the new list.

7. Francisco, Mildred 7.____
   A. Right before Mark Grant
   B. Right after Marissa Grantt
   C. Right before Alison Marrow
   D. Right after Kendall Asanti

Questions 8-10.

DIRECTIONS: In answering Questions 8 through 10, compare each pair of names and addresses. Indicate whether they are the same or different in any way.

8. William H. Pratt, J.D. / Attourney at Law — William H. Pratt, J.D. / Attorney at Law 8.____
   A. No differences
   B. 1 difference
   C. 2 differences
   D. 3 differences

9. 1303 Theater Drive,; Apt. 3-B — 1330 Theatre Drive,; Apt. 3-B 9.____
   A. No differences
   B. 1 difference
   C. 2 differences
   D. 3 differences

10. Petersdorff, Briana and Mary — Petersdorff, Briana and Mary 10.____
   A. No differences
   B. 1 difference
   C. 2 differences
   D. 3 differences

11. Which of the following words, if any, are misspelled? 11.____
   A. Affordable
   B. Circumstansial
   C. Legalese
   D. None of the above

Questions 12-13.

DIRECTIONS: Questions 12 and 13 are to be answered on the basis of the following table.

Standardized Test Results for High School Students in District #1230

	English	Math	Science	Reading
High School 1	21	22	15	18
High School 2	12	16	13	15
High School 3	16	18	21	17
High School 4	19	14	15	16

The scores for each high school in the district were averaged out and listed for each subject tested. Scores of 0-10 are significantly below College Readiness Standards. 11-15 are below College Readiness, 16-20 meet College Readiness, and 21-25 are above College Readiness.

12. If the high schools need to meet or exceed in at least half the categories in order to NOT be considered "at risk," which schools are considered "at risk"? 12.____
    A. High School 2
    B. High School 3
    C. High School 4
    D. Both A and C

13. What percentage of subjects did the district as a whole meet or exceed College Readiness standards? 13.____
    A. 25%
    B. 50%
    C. 75%
    D. 100%

Questions 14-15.

DIRECTIONS: Questions 14 and 15 are to be answered on the basis of the following information.

You have seven employees working as a part of your team: Austin, Emily, Jeremy, Christina, Martin, Harriet, and Steve. You have just sent an e-mail informing them that there will be a mandatory training session next week. To ensure that work still gets done, you are offering the training twice during the week: once on Tuesday and also on Thursday. This way half the employees will still be working while the other half attend the training. The only other issue is that Jeremy doesn't work on Tuesdays and Harriet doesn't work on Thursdays due to compressed work schedules.

14. Which of the following is a possible attendance roster for the first training session? 14.____
    A. Emily, Jeremy, Steve
    B. Steve, Christina, Harriet
    C. Harriet, Jeremy, Austin
    D. Steve, Martin, Jeremy

15. If Harriet, Christina, and Steve attend the training session on Tuesday, which of the following is a possible roster for Thursday's training session? 15.____
    A. Jeremy, Emily, and Austin
    B. Emily, Martin, and Harriet
    C. Austin, Christina, and Emily
    D. Jeremy, Emily, and Steve

Questions 16-20.

DIRECTIONS: In answering Questions 16 through 20, you will be given a word and will need to choose the answer choice that is MOST similar or different to the word.

16. Which word means the SAME as *annual*? 16.____
    A. Monthly
    B. Usually
    C. Yearly
    D. Constantly

17. Which word means the SAME as *effort*? 17.____
    A. Energy
    B. Equate
    C. Cherish
    D. Commence

18. Which word means the OPPOSITE of *forlorn*? 18.____
    A. Neglected
    B. Lethargy
    C. Optimistic
    D. Astonished

19. Which word means the SAME as *risk*? 19.____
    A. Admire
    B. Hazard
    C. Limit
    D. Hesitant

20. Which word means the OPPOSITE of *translucent*? 20.____
    A. Opaque B. Transparent C. Luminous D. Introverted

21. Last year, Jamie's annual salary was $50,000. Her boss called her today to inform her that she would receive a 20% raise for the upcoming year. How much more money will Jamie receive next year? 21.____
    A. $60,000 B. $10,000 C. $1,000 D. $51,000

22. You and a co-worker work for a temp hiring agency as part of their office staff. You both are given 6 days off per month. How many days off are you and your co-worker given in a year? 22.____
    A. 24 B. 72 C. 144 D. 48

23. If Margot makes $34,000 per year and she works 40 hours per week for all 52 weeks, what is her hourly rate? 23.____
    A. $16.34/hour B. $17.00/hour C. $15.54/hour D. $13.23/hour

24. How many dimes are there in $175.00? 24.____
    A. 175 B. 1,750 C. 3,500 D. 17,500

25. If Janey is three times as old as Emily, and Emily is 3, how old is Janey? 25.____
    A. 6 B. 9 C. 12 D. 15

KEY (CORRECT ANSWERS)

1. C
2. D
3. A
4. B
5. B

6. C
7. A
8. B
9. C
10. A

11. B
12. A
13. D
14. B
15. A

16. C
17. A
18. C
19. B
20. A

21. B
22. C
23. A
24. B
25. B

TEST 2

DIRECTIONS: Each question or incomplete statement is followed by several suggested answers or completions. Select the one that BEST answers the question or completes the statement. *PRINT THE LETTER OF THE CORRECT ANSWER IN THE SPACE AT THE RIGHT.*

Questions 1-6.

DIRECTIONS: Questions 1 through 6 are to be answered on the basis of the following information.

item	name of item to be ordered
quantity	minimum number that can be ordered
beginning amount	amount in stock at start of month
amount received	amount receiving during month
ending amount	amount in stock at end of month
amount used	amount used during month
amount to order	will need at least as much of each item as used in the previous month
unit price	cost of each unit of an item
total price	total price for the order

Item	Quantity	Beginning	Received	Ending	Amount Used	Amount to Order	Unit Price	Total Price
Pens	10	22	10	8	24	20	$0.11	$2.20
Spiral notebooks	8	30	13	12			$0.25	
Binder clips	2 boxes	3 boxes	1 box	1 box			$1.79	
Sticky notes	3 packs	12 packs	4 packs	2 packs			$1.29	
Dry erase markers	1 pack (dozen)	34 markers	8 markers	40 markers			$16.49	
Ink cartridges (printer)	1 cartridge	3 cartridges	1 cartridge	2 cartridges			$79.99	
Folders	10 folders	25 folders	15 folders	10 folders			$1.08	

1. How many packs of sticky notes were used during the month? 1.____
   A. 16 B. 10 C. 12 D. 14

2. How many folders need to be ordered for next month? 2.____
   A. 15 B. 20 C. 30 D. 40

3. What is the total price of notebooks that you will need to order? 3.____
   A. $6.00 B. $0.25 C. $4.50 D. $2.75

4. Which of the following will you spend the second most money on? 4.____
   A. Ink cartridges B. Dry erase markers
   C. Sticky notes D. Binder clips

5. How many packs of dry erase markers should you order? 5.____
   A. 1 B. 8 C. 12 D. 0

6. What will be the total price of the file folders you order? 6.____
   A. $20.16   B. $21.60   C. $10.80   D. $4.32

Questions 7-11.

DIRECTIONS: Questions 7 through 11 are to be answered on the basis of the following table.

Number of Car Accidents, By Location and Cause, for 2014						
	Location 1		Location 2		Location 3	
Cause	Number	Percent	Number	Percent	Number	Percent
Severe Weather	10		25		30	
Excessive Speeding	20	40	5		10	
Impaired Driving	15		15	25	8	
Miscellaneous	5		15		2	4
TOTALS	50	100	60	100	50	100

7. Which of the following is the third highest cause of accidents for all three locations? 7.____
   A. Severe Weather   B. Impaired Driving
   C. Miscellaneous   D. Excessive Speeding

8. The average number of Severe Weather accidents per week at Location 3 for the year (52 weeks) was MOST NEARLY 8.____
   A. 0.57   B. 30   C. 1   D. 1.25

9. Which location had the LARGEST percentage of accidents caused by Impaired Driving? 9.____
   A. 1   B. 2   C. 3   D. Both A and B

10. If one-third of the accidents at all three locations resulted in at least one fatality, what is the LEAST amount of deaths caused by accidents last year? 10.____
   A. 60   B. 106   C. 66   D. 53

11. What is the percentage of accidents caused by miscellaneous means from all three locations in 2014? 11.____
   A. 5%   B. 10%   C. 13%   D. 25%

12. How many pairs of the following groups of letters are exactly alike? 12.____

ACDOBJ	ACDBOJ
HEWBWR	HEWRWB
DEERVS	DEERVS
BRFQSX	BRFQSX
WEYRVB	WEYRVB
SPQRZA	SQRPZA

   A. 2   B. 3   C. 4   D. 5

Questions 13-19.

DIRECTIONS: Questions 13 through 19 are to be answered on the basis of the following information.

In 2012, the most current information on the American population was finished. The information was compiled by 200 volunteers in each of the 50 states. The territory of Puerto Rico, a sovereign of the United States, had 25 people assigned to compile data. In February of 2010, volunteers in each state and sovereign began collecting information. In Puerto Rico, data collection finished by January 31st, 2011, while work in the United States was completed on June 30, 2012. Each volunteer gathered data on the population of their state or sovereign. When the information was compiled, volunteers sent reports to the nation's capital, Washington, D.C. Each volunteer worked 20 hours per month and put together 10 reports per month. After the data was compiled in total, 50 people reviewed the data and worked from January 2012 to December 2012.

13. How many reports were generated from February 2010 to April 2010 in Illinois and Ohio? 13.____
A. 3,000 B. 6,000 C. 12,000 D. 15,000

14. How many volunteers in total collected population data in January 2012? 14.____
A. 10,000 B. 2,000 C. 225 D. 200

15. How many reports were put together in May 2012? 15.____
A. 2,000 B. 50,000 C. 100,000 D. 100,250

16. How many hours did the Puerto Rican volunteers work in the fall (September-November)? 16.____
A. 60 B. 500 C. 1,500 D. 0

17. How many workers were compiling or reviewing data in July 2012? 17.____
A. 25 B. 50 C. 200 D. 250

18. What was the total amount of hours worked by Nevada volunteers in July 2010? 18.____
A. 500 B. 4,000 C. 4,500 D. 5,000

19. How many reviewers worked in January 2013? 19.____
A. 75 B. 50 C. 0 D. 25

20. John has to file 10 documents per shelf. How many documents would it take for John to fill 40 shelves? 20.____
A. 40 B. 400 C. 4,500 D. 5,000

21. Jill wants to travel from New York City to Los Angeles by bike, which is approximately 2,772 miles. How many miles per day would Jill need to average if she wanted to complete the trip in 4 weeks? 21.____
A. 100 B. 89 C. 99 D. 94

22. If there are 24 CPU's and only 7 monitors, how many more monitors do you need to have the same amount of monitors as CPU's? 22.____
    A. Not enough information B. 17
    C. 31 D. 0

23. If Gerry works 5 days a week and 8 hours each day, and John works 3 days a week and 10 hours each day, how many more hours per year will Gerry work than John? 23.____
    A. They work the same amount of hours.
    B. 450
    C. 520
    D. 832

24. Jimmy gets transferred to a new office. The new office has 25 employees, but only 16 are there due to a blizzard. How many coworkers was Jimmy able to meet on his first day? 24.____
    A. 16 B. 25 C. 9 D. 7

25. If you do a fundraiser for charities in your area and raise $500 total, how much would you give to each charity if you were donating equal amounts to 3 of them? 25.____
    A. $250.00 B. $167.77 C. $50.00 D. $111.11

KEY (CORRECT ANSWERS)

1.	D	11.	C
2.	B	12.	B
3.	A	13.	C
4.	C	14.	A
5.	D	15.	C
6.	B	16.	C
7.	D	17.	B
8.	A	18.	B
9.	A	19.	C
10.	D	20.	B

21.	C
22.	B
23.	C
24.	A
25.	B

TEST 3

DIRECTIONS: Each question or incomplete statement is followed by several suggested answers or completions. Select the one that BEST answers the question or completes the statement. *PRINT THE LETTER OF THE CORRECT ANSWER IN THE SPACE AT THE RIGHT.*

Questions 1-3.

DIRECTIONS: In answering Questions 1 through 3, choose the correctly spelled word.

1. A. allusion B. alusion C. allusien D. allution 1.____

2. A. altitude B. alltitude C. atlitude D. altlitude 2.____

3. A. althogh B. allthough C. althrough D. although 3.____

Questions 4-9.

DIRECTIONS: In answering Questions 4 through 9, choose the answer that BEST completes the analogy.

4. Odometer is to mileage as compass is to 4.____
   A. speed B. needle C. hiking D. direction

5. Marathon is to race as hibernation is to 5.____
   A. winter B. dream C. sleep D. bear

6. Cup is to coffee as bowl is to 6.____
   A. dish B. spoon C. food D. soup

7. Flow is to river as stagnant is to 7.____
   A. pool B. rain C. stream D. canal

8. Paw is to cat as hoof is to 8.____
   A. lamb B. horse C. lion D. elephant

9. Architect is to building as sculptor is to 9.____
   A. museum B. chisel C. stone D. statue

Questions 10-14.

DIRECTIONS: Questions 10 through 14 are to be answered on the basis of the following graph.

Population of Carroll City Broken Down by Age and Gender (in Thousands)			
Age	Female	Male	Total
Under 15	60	60	120
15-23		22	
24-33		20	44
34-43	13	18	31
44-53	20		67
64 and Over	65	65	130
TOTAL	230	232	462

10. How many people in the city are between the ages of 15-23? 10.____
    A. 70 B. 46,000 C. 70,000 D. 225,000

11. Approximately what percentage of the total population of the city was female aged 24-33? 11.____
    A. 10% B. 5% C. 15% D. 25%

12. If 33% of the males have a job and 55% of females don't have a job, which of the following statements is TRUE? 12.____
    A. Males have approximately 2,600 more jobs than females.
    B. Females have approximately 49,000 more jobs than males.
    C. Females have approximately 26,000 more jobs than males.
    D. None of the above statements are true.

13. How many females between the ages of 15-23 live in Carroll City? 13.____
    A. 67,000 B. 24,000 C. 48,000 D. 91,000

14. Assume all males 44-53 living in Carroll City are employed. If two-thirds of males age 44-53 work jobs outside of Carroll City, how many work within city limits? 14.____
    A. 31,333
    B. 15,667
    C. 47,000
    D. Cannot answer the question with the information provided

Questions 15-16.

DIRECTIONS: Questions 15 and 16 are labeled as shown. Alphabetize them for filing. Choose the answer that correctly shows the order.

15. (1) AED 15.____
(2) OOS
(3) FOA
(4) DOM
(5) COB

A. 2-5-4-3-2 B. 1-4-5-2-3 C. 1-5-4-2-3 D. 1-5-4-3-2

16. Alphabetize the names of the people. Last names are given last. 16.____
(1) Lindsey Jamestown
(2) Jane Alberta
(3) Ally Jamestown
(4) Allison Johnston
(5) Lyle Moreno

A. 2-1-3-4-5 B. 3-4-2-1-5 C. 2-3-1-4-5 D. 4-3-2-1-5

17. Which of the following words is misspelled? 17.____
A. disgust B. whisper
C. locale D. none of the above

Questions 18-21.

DIRECTIONS: Questions 18 through 21 are to be answered on the basis of the following list of employees.

Robertson, Aaron
Bacon, Gina
Jerimiah, Trace
Gillette, Stanley
Jacks, Sharon

18. Which employee name would come in third in alphabetized list? 18.____
A. Robertson, Aaron B. Jerimiah, Trace
C. Gillette, Stanley D. Jacks, Sharon

19. Which employee's first name starts with the letter in the alphabet that is five letters after the first letter of their last name? 19.____
A. Jerimiah, Trace B. Bacon, Gina
C. Jacks, Sharon D. Gillette, Stanley

20. How many employees have last names that are exactly five letters long? 20.____
A. 1 B. 2 C. 3 D. 4

21. How many of the employees have either a first or last name that starts with the letter "G"? 21.____
A. 1 B. 2 C. 4 D. 5

Questions 22-25.

DIRECTIONS: Questions 22 through 25 are to be answered on the basis of the following chart.

Bicycle Sales (Model #34JA32)							
Country	May	June	July	August	September	October	Total
Germany	34	47	45	54	56	60	296
Britain	40	44	36	47	47	46	260
Ireland	37	32	32	32	34	33	200
Portugal	14	14	14	16	17	14	89
Italy	29	29	28	31	29	31	177
Belgium	22	24	24	26	25	23	144
Total	176	198	179	206	208	207	1166

22. What percentage of the overall total was sold to the German importer? 22.____
A. 25.3% B. 22% C. 24.1% D. 23%

23. What percentage of the overall total was sold in September? 23.____
A. 24.1% B. 25.6% C. 17.9% D. 24.6%

24. What is the average number of units per month imported into Belgium over the first four months shown? 24.____
A. 26 B. 20 C. 24 D. 31

25. If you look at the three smallest importers, what is their total import percentage? 25.____
A. 35.1% B. 37.1% C. 40% D. 28%

KEY (CORRECT ANSWERS)

1. A
2. A
3. D
4. D
5. C

6. D
7. A
8. B
9. D
10. C

11. B
12. C
13. C
14. B
15. D

16. C
17. D
18. D
19. B
20. B

21. B
22. A
23. C
24. C
25. A

TEST 4

DIRECTIONS: Each question or incomplete statement is followed by several suggested answers or completions. Select the one that BEST answers the question or completes the statement. *PRINT THE LETTER OF THE CORRECT ANSWER IN THE SPACE AT THE RIGHT.*

Questions 1-6.

DIRECTIONS: In answering Questions 1 through 6, choose the sentence that represents the BEST example of English grammar.

1. A. Joey and me want to go on a vacation next week. 1.____
   B. Gary told Jim he would need to take some time off.
   C. If turning six years old, Jim's uncle would teach Spanish to him.
   D. Fax a copy of your resume to Ms. Perez and me.

2. A. Jerry stood in line for almost two hours. 2.____
   B. The reaction to my engagement was less exciting than I thought it would be.
   C. Carlos and me have done great work on this project.
   D. Two parts of the speech needs to be revised before tomorrow.

3. A. Arriving home, the alarm was tripped. 3.____
   B. Jonny is regarded as a stand up guy, a responsible parent, and he doesn't give up until a task is finished.
   C. Each employee must submit a drug test each month.
   D. One of the documents was incinerated in the explosion.

4. A. As soon as my parents get home, I told them I finished all of my chores. 4.____
   B. I asked my teacher to send me my missing work, check my absences, and how did I do on my test.
   C. Matt attempted to keep it concealed from Jenny and me.
   D. If Mary or him cannot get work done on time, I will have to split them up.

5. A. Driving to work, the traffic report warned him of an accident on Highway 47. 5.____
   B. Jimmy has performed well this season.
   C. Since finishing her degree, several job offers have been given to Cam.
   D. Our boss is creating unstable conditions for we employees.

6. A. The thief was described as a tall man with a wiry mustache weighing approximately 150 pounds. 6.____
   B. She gave Patrick and I some more time to finish our work.
   C. One of the books that he ordered was damaged in shipping.
   D. While talking on the rotary phone, the car Jim was driving skidded off the road.

Questions 7-9.

DIRECTIONS: Questions 7 through 9 are to be answered on the basis of the following graph.

Ice Lake Frozen Flight (2002-2013)		
Year	Number of Participants	Temperature (Fahrenheit)
2002	22	4°
2003	50	33°
2004	69	18°
2005	104	22°
2006	108	24°
2007	288	33°
2008	173	9°
2009	598	39°
2010	698	26°
2011	696	30°
2012	777	28°
2013	578,	32°

7. Which two year span had the LARGEST difference between temperatures? 7.____
   A. 2002 and 2003
   B. 2011 and 2012
   C. 2008 and 2009
   D. 2003 and 2004

8. How many total people participated in the years after the temperature reached at least 29°? 8.____
   A. 2,295
   B. 1,717
   C. 2,210
   D. 4,543

9. In 2007, the event saw 288 participants, while in 2008 that number dropped to 173. Which of the following reasons BEST explains the drop in participants? 9.____
   A. The event had not been going on that long and people didn't know about it.
   B. The lake water wasn't cold enough to have people jump in.
   C. The temperature was too cold for many people who would have normally participated.
   D. None of the above reasons explain the drop in participants.

10. In the following list of numbers, how many times does 4 come just after 2 when 2 comes just after an odd number? 10.____
    2365247653898632488572486392424
    A. 2
    B. 3
    C. 4
    D. 5

11. Which choice below lists the letter that is as far after B as S is after N in the alphabet? 11.____
    A. G
    B. H
    C. I
    D. J

Questions 12-15.

DIRECTIONS: Questions 12 through 15 are to be answered on the basis of the following directory and list of changes.

Directory		
Name	Emp. Type	Position
Julie Taylor	Warehouse	Packer
James King	Office	Administrative Assistant
John Williams	Office	Salesperson
Ray Moore	Warehouse	Maintenance
Kathleen Byrne	Warehouse	Supervisor
Amy Jones	Office	Salesperson
Paul Jonas	Office	Salesperson
Lisa Wong	Warehouse	Loader
Eugene Lee	Office	Accountant
Bruce Lavine	Office	Manager
Adam Gates	Warehouse	Packer
Will Suter	Warehouse	Packer
Gary Lorper	Office	Accountant
Jon Adams	Office	Salesperson
Susannah Harper	Office	Salesperson

Directory Updates:

- Employee e-mail addresses will adhere to the following guidelines: lastnamefirstname@apexindustries.com (ex. Susannah Harper is harpersusannah@apexindustries.com). Currently, employees in the warehouse share one e-mail, distribution@apexindustries.com.
- The "Loader" position will now be referred to as "Specialist I"
- Adam Gates has accepted a Supervisor position within the Warehouse and is no longer a Packer. All warehouse employees report to the two Supervisors and all office employees report to the Manager.

12. Amy Jones tried to send an e-mail to Adam Gates, but it wouldn't send. Which of the following offers the BEST explanation? 12.____
    A. Amy put Adam's first name first and then his last name.
    B. Adam doesn't check his e-mail, so he wouldn't know if he received the e-mail or not.
    C. Adam does not have his own e-mail.
    D. Office employees are not allowed to send e-mails to each other.

13. How many Packers currently work for Apex Industries? 13.____
    A. 2 B. 3 C. 4 D. 5

14. What position does Lisa Wong currently hold? 14.____
    A. Specialist I B. Secretary
    C. Administrative Assistant D. Loader

15. If an employee wanted to contact the office manager, which of the following e-mails should the e-mail be sent to? 15.____
    A. officemanager@apexindustries.com
    B. brucelavine@apexindustries.com
    C. lavinebruce@apexindustries.com
    D. distribution@apexindustries.com

Questions 16-19.

DIRECTIONS: In answering Questions 16 through 19, compare the three names, numbers or addresses.

16. Smiley Yarnell Smiley Yarnel Smily Yarnell 16.____
    A. All three are exactly alike.
    B. The first and second are exactly alike.
    C. The second and third are exactly alike.
    D. All three are different.

17. 1583 Theater Drive 1583 Theater Drive 1583 Theatre Drive 17.____
    A. All three are exactly alike.
    B. The first and second are exactly alike.
    C. The second and third are exactly alike.
    D. All three are different.

18. 3341893212 3341893212 3341893212 18.____
    A. All three are exactly alike.
    B. The first and second are exactly alike.
    C. The second and third are exactly alike.
    D. All three are different.

19. Douglass Watkins Douglas Watkins Douglass Watkins 19.____
    A. All three are exactly alike.
    B. The first and third are exactly alike.
    C. The second and third are exactly alike.
    D. All three are different.

Questions 20-24.

DIRECTIONS: In answering Questions 20 through 24, you will be presented with a word. Choose the synonym that BEST represents the word in question.

20. Flexible 20.____
    A. delicate B. inflammable C. strong D. pliable

21. Alternative 21.____
    A. choice B. moderate C. lazy D. value

22. Corroborate — 22.____
   A. examine B. explain C. verify D. explain

23. Respiration — 23.____
   A. recovery B. breathing C. sweating D. selfish

24. Negligent — 24.____
   A. lazy B. moderate C. hopeless D. lax

25. Plumber is to Wrench as Painter is to — 25.____
   A. pipe B. shop C. hammer D. brush

KEY (CORRECT ANSWERS)

1.	D	11.	A
2.	A	12.	C
3.	D	13.	A
4.	C	14.	A
5.	B	15.	C
6.	C	16.	D
7.	C	17.	B
8.	B	18.	A
9.	C	19.	B
10.	C	20.	D

21.	A
22.	C
23.	B
24.	D
25.	D

NAME AND NUMBER CHECKING

EXAMINATION SECTION

TEST 1

DIRECTIONS: This test is designed to measure your speed/and accuracy. You are urged to work both quickly and accurately and to do correctly as many lists as you can in the time allowed. The test consists of lists or pairs of names and numbers. Count the number of IDENTICAL pairs in each list. Then, select the correct number, 1, 2, 3, 4, 5, and indicate your choice in the space at the right. Two sample questions are presented for your guidance, together with the correct solutions.

SAMPLE LIST A

Adelphi College	– Adelphia College
Braxton Corp	– Braxeton Corp.
Wassaic State School	– Wassaic State School
Central Islip State Hospital	– Central Isllip State Hospital
Greenwich House	– Greenwich House

NOTE: There are only two correct pairs—Wassaic State School and Greenwich House. Therefore, the CORRECT answer is 2.

SAMPLE LIST B

78453694	– 78453684
784530	– 784530
533	– 534
67845	– 67845
2368745	– 2368755

NOTE: There are only two correct pairs—784530 and 67845. Therefore, the CORRECT answer is 2.

LIST 1 1.____

98654327	- 98654327
74932564	- 7492564
61438652	- 61438652
01297653	- 01287653
1865439765	- 1865439765

LIST 2 2.____

478362	- 478363
278354792	- 278354772
9327	- 9327
297384625	- 27384625
6428156	- 6428158

LIST 3		3.____
Abbey House	- Abbey House	
Actor's Fund Home	- Actor's Fund Home	
Adrian Memorial	- Adrian Memorial	
A. Clayton Powell Home	- Clayton Powell House	
Abbot E. Kittredge Club	- Abbott E. Kitteredge Club	

LIST 4		4.____
3682	- 3692	
21937453829	- 31927453829	
723	- 733	
2763920	- 2763920	
47293	- 47293	

LIST 5		5.____
Adra House	- Adra House	
Adolescents' Court	- Adolescents' Court	
Cliff Villa	- Cliff Villa	
Clark Neighborhood House	- Clark Neighborhood House	
Alma Mathews House	- Alma Mathews House	

LIST 6		6.____
28734291	- 28734271	
63810263849	- 63810263846	
26831027	- 26831027	
368291	- 368291	
7238102637	- 7238102637	

LIST 7		7.____
Albion State T.S.	- Albion State T.C.	
Clara de Hirsch Home	- Clara De Hirsch Home	
Alice Carrington Royce	- Alice Carington Royce	
Alice Chopin Nursery	- Alice Chapin Nursery	
Lighthouse Eye Clinic	- Lighthouse Eye Clinic	

LIST 8		8.____
327	- 329	
712438291026	- 712438291026	
2753829142	- 275382942	
826287	- 826289	
26435162839	- 26435162839	

LIST 9		9.____
Letchworth Village	- Letchworth Village	
A.A.A.E. Inc.	- A.A.A.E. Inc.	
Clear Pool Camp	- Clear Pool Camp	
A.M.M.L.A. Inc.	- A.M.M.L.A. Inc.	
J.G. Harbard	- J.G. Harbord	

LIST 10		10.____
8254	- 8256	
2641526	- 2641526	
4126389012	- 4126389102	
725	- 725	
76253917287	- 76253917287	

LIST 11		11.____
Attica State Prison	- Attica State Prison	
Nellie Murrah	- Nellie Murrah	
Club Marshall	- Club Marshal	
Assissium Casea-Maria	- Assissium Casa-Maria	
The Homestead	- The Homestead	

LIST 12		12.____
2691	- 2691	
623819253627	- 623819253629	
28637	- 28937	
278392736	- 278392736	
52739	- 52739	

LIST 13		13.____
A.I.C.P. Boys Camp	- A.I.C.P. Boy's Camp	
Einar Chrystie	- Einar Christyie	
Astoria Center	- Astoria Center	
G. Frederick Brown	- G. Federick Browne	
Vacation Service	- Vacation Services	

LIST 14		14.____
728352689	- 728352688	
643728	- 643728	
37829176	- 37827196	
8425367	- 8425369	
65382018	- 65382018	

LIST 15		15.____
E.S. Streim	- E.S. Strim	
Charles E. Higgins	- Charles E. Higgins	
Baluvelt, N.Y.	- Blauwelt, N.Y.	
Roberta Magdalen	- Roberto Magdalen	
Ballard School	- Ballard School	

LIST 16		16.____
7382	- 7392	
281374538299	- 291374538299	
623	- 633	
6273730	- 6273730	
63392	- 63392	

LIST 17		17.____
Orrin Otis	- Orrin Otis	
Barat Settlement	- Barat Settlemen	
Emmanuel House	- Emmanuel House	
William T. McCreery	- William T. McCreery	
Seamen's Home	- Seaman's Home	
LIST 18		18.____
72824391	- 72834371	
3729106237	- 37291106237	
82620163849	- 82620163846	
37638921	- 37638921	
82631027	- 82631027	
LIST 19		19.____
Commonwealth Fund	- Commonwealth Fund	
Anne Johnsen	- Anne Johnson	
Bide-A-Wee Home	- Bide-a-Wee Home	
Riverdale-on-Hudson	- Riverdal-on-Hudson	
Bialystoker Home	- Bailystoker Home	
LIST 20		20.____
9271	- 9271	
392918352627	- 392018852629	
72637	- 72637	
927392736	- 927392736	
92739	- 92739	
LIST 21		21.____
Charles M. Stump	- Charles M. Stump	
Bourne Workshop	- Buorne Workshop	
B'nai Bi'rith	- B'nai Brith	
Poppenhuesen Institute	- Poppenheusen Institute	
Consular Service	- Consular Service	
LIST 22		22.____
927352689	- 927352688	
647382	- 648382	
93729176	- 93727196	
649536718	- 649536718	
5835367	- 5835369	
LIST 23		23.____
L.S. Bestend	- L.S. Bestent	
Hirsch Mfg. Co.	- Hircsh Mfg. Co.	
F.H. Storrs	- F.P. Storrs	
Camp Wassaic	- Camp Wassaic	
George Ballingham	- George Ballingham	

LIST 24 24.____

372846392048	- 372846392048
334	- 334
7283524678	- 7283524678
7283	- 7283
7283629372	- 7283629372

LIST 25 25.____

Dr. Stiles Company	- Dr. Stills Company
Frances Hunsdon	- Frances Hunsdon
Northrop Barrert	- Nothrup Barrent
J.D. Brunjes	- J.D. Brunjes
Theo. Claudel & Co.	- Theo. Claudel co.

KEY (CORRECT ANSWERS)

1. 3
2. 1
3. 2
4. 2
5. 5
6. 3
7. 1
8. 2
9. 4
10. 3
11. 3
12. 3
13. 1
14. 2
15. 2
16. 2
17. 3
18. 2
19. 2
20. 4
21. 2
22. 1
23. 2
24. 5
25. 2

TEST 2

DIRECTIONS: This test is designed to measure your speed/and accuracy. You are urged to work both quickly and accurately and to do correctly as many lists as you can in the time allowed. The test consists of lists or pairs of names and numbers. Count the number of IDENTICAL pairs in each list. Then, select the correct number, 1, 2, 3, 4, 5, and indicate your choice in the space at the right.

LIST 1 — 1.____

82728 - 82738
82736292637 - 82736292639
728 - 738
83926192527 - 83726192529
82736272 - 82736272

LIST 2 — 2.____

L. Pietri - L. Pietri
Mathewson, L.F. - Mathewson, L.F.
Funk & Wagnall - Funk & Wagnalls
Shimizu, Sojio - Shimizu, Sojio
Filing Equipment Bureau - Filing Equipment Buraeu

LIST 3 — 3.____

63801829374 - 63801839474
283577657 - 283577657
65689 - 65689
3457892026 - 3547893026
2779 - 2778

LIST 4 — 4.____

August Caille - August Caille
The Well-Fare Service - The Wel-Fare Service
K.L.M. Process co. - R.L.M. Process Co.
Merrill Littell - Merrill Littell
Dodd & Sons - Dodd & Son

LIST 5 — 5.____

998745732 - 998745733
723 - 723
463849102983 - 463849102983
8570 - 8570
279012 - 279012

LIST 6 — 6.____

M.A. Wender - M.A. Winder
Minneapolis Supply Co. - Minneapolis Supply Co.
Beverly Hills Corp - Beverley Hills Corp.
Trafalgar Square - Trafalgar Square
Phifer, D.T. - Phiefer, D.T.

LIST 7		7.____
7834629	- 7834629	
3549806746	- 3549806746	
97802564	- 97892564	
689246	- 688246	
2578024683	- 2578024683	
LIST 8		8.____
Scadrons'	- Scadrons'	
Gensen & Bro.	- Genson & Bro.	
Firestone Co.	- Firestone Co.	
H.L. Eklund	- H.L. Eklund	
Oleomargarine Co.	- Oleomargarine Co.	
LIST 9		9.____
782039485618	- 782039485618	
53829172639	- 63829172639	
892	- 892	
82937482	- 829374820	
52937456	- 53937456	
LIST 10		10.____
First Nat'l Bank	- First Nat'l Bank	
Sedgwick Machine Works	- Sedgewick Machine Works	
Hectographia Co.	- Hectographia Corp.	
Levet Bros.	- Levet Bros.	
Multistamp Co., Inc.	- Multistamp Co., Inc.	
LIST 11		11.____
7293	- 7293	
6382910293	- 6382910292	
981928374012	- 981928374912	
58293	- 58393	
18203649271	- 283019283745	
LIST 12		12.____
Lowrey Lb'r Co.	- Lowrey Lb'r Co.	
Fidelity Service	- Fidelity Service	
Reumann, J.A.	- Reumann, J.A.	
Duophoto Ltd.	- Duophotos Ltd.	
John Jarratt	- John Jaratt	
LIST 13		13.____
6820384	- 6820384	
383019283745	- 383019283745	
63927102	- 63928102	
91029354829	- 91029354829	
58291728	- 58291728	

LIST 14		14.____
Standard Press Co.	- Standard Press Co.	
Reliant Mf'g. Co.	- Relant Mf'g Co.	
M.C. Lynn	- M.C. Lynn	
J. Fredericks Company	- G. Fredericks Company	
Wandermann, B.S.	- Wanderman, B.S.	
LIST 15		15.____
4283910293	- 4283010203	
992018273648	- 992018273848	
620	- 629	
752937273	- 752937373	
5392	- 5392	
LIST 16		16.____
Waldorf Hotel	- Waldorf Hotel	
Aaron Machinery Co.	- Aaron Machinery Co.	
Caroline Ann Locke	- Caroline Ane Locke	
McCabe Mfg. Co.	- McCabe Mfg. Co.	
R.L. Landres	- R.L. Landers	
LIST 17		17.____
68391028364	- 68391028394	
68293	- 68293	
739201	- 739201	
72839201	- 72839211	
739917	- 739719	
LIST 18		18.____
Balsam M.M.	- Balsamm, M.M.	
Steinway & Co.	- Stienway & M. Co.	
Eugene Elliott	- Eugene A. Elliott	
Leonard Loan Co.	- Leonard Loan Co.	
Frederick Morgan	- Frederick Morgen	
LIST 19		19.____
8929	- 9820	
392836472829	- 392836572829	
462	- 4622039271	
827	- 2039276837	
53829	- 54829	
LIST 20		20.____
Danielson's Hofbrau	- Danielson's Hafbrau	
Edward A. Truarme	- Edward A. Truame	
Insulite Co.	- Insulite Co.	
Reisler Shoe Corp.	- Rielser Shoe Corp.	
L.L. Thompson	- L.L. Thompson	

LIST 21		21.____
92839102837	- 92839102837	
58891028	- 58891028	
7291728	- 7291928	
272839102839	- 272839102839	
428192	- 428102	
LIST 22		22.____
K.L. Veiller	- K.L. Veiller	
Webster, Roy	- Webster, Ray	
Drasner Spring Co.	- Drasner Spring Co.	
Edward J. Cravenport	- Edward J. Cravanport	
Harold Field	- Harold A. Field	
LIST 23		23.____
2293	- 2293	
4283910293	- 5382910292	
871928374012	- 871928374912	
68293	- 68393	
8120364927	- 81293649271	
LIST 24		24.____
Tappe, Inc	- Tappe, Inc.	
A.M. Wentingworth	- A.M. Wentinworth	
Scott A. Elliott	- Scott A. Elliott	
Echeverria Corp.	- Echeverria Corp.	
Bradford Victor Company	- Bradford Victer Company	
LIST 25		25.____
4820384	- 4820384	
393019283745	- 283919283745	
63917102	- 63927102	
91029354829	- 91029354829	
48291728	- 48291728	

KEY (CORRECT ANSWERS)

1.	1	11.	1
2.	3	12.	3
3.	2	13.	4
4.	2	14.	2
5.	4	15.	1
6.	2	16.	3
7.	3	17.	2
8.	4	18.	1
9.	2	19.	1
10.	3	20.	2

21.	3
22.	2
23.	1
24.	2
25.	4

PHILOSOPHY, PRINCIPLES, PRACTICES, AND TECHNICS OF SUPERVISION, ADMINISTRATION, MANAGEMENT, AND ORGANIZATION

TABLE OF CONTENTS

PHILOSOPHY, PRINCIPLES, PRACTICES, AND TECHNICS
OF
SUPERVISION, ADMINISTRATION, MANAGEMENT, AND ORGANIZATION

MEANING OF SUPERVISION

The extension of the democratic philosophy has been accompanied by an extension in the scope of supervision. Modern leaders and supervisors no longer think of supervision in the narrow sense of being confined chiefly to visiting employees, supplying materials, or rating the staff. They regard supervision as being intimately related to all the concerned agencies of society, they speak of the supervisor's function in terms of "growth," rather than the "improvement" of employees.

This modern concept of supervision may be defined as follows: Supervision is leadership and the development of leadership within groups which are cooperatively engaged in inspection, research, training, guidance, and evaluation.

THE OLD AND THE NEW SUPERVISION

TRADITIONAL
1. Inspection
2. Focused on the employee
3. Visitation
4. Random and haphazard
5. Imposed and authoritarian
6. One person usually

MODERN
1. Study and analysis
2. Focused on aims, materials, methods, supervisors, employees, environment
3. Demonstrations, intervisitation, workshops, directed reading, bulletins, etc.
4. Definitely organized and planned (scientific)
5. Cooperative and democratic
6. Many persons involved (creative)

THE EIGHT (8) BASIC PRINCIPLES OF THE NEW SUPERVISION

I. Principle of Responsibility
Authority to act and responsibility for acting must be joined.
A. If you give responsibility, give authority.
B. Define employee duties clearly.
C. Protect employees from criticism by others.
D. Recognize the rights as well as obligations of employees.
E. Achieve the aims of a democratic society insofar as it is possible within the area of your work.
F. Establish a situation favorable to training and learning.
G. Accept ultimate responsibility for everything done in your section, unit, office, division, department.
H. Good administration and good supervision are inseparable.

II. Principle of Authority

The success of the supervisor is measured by the extent to which the power of authority is not used.

A. Exercise simplicity and informality in supervision
B. Use the simplest machinery of supervision
C. If it is good for the organization as a whole, it is probably justified.
D. Seldom be arbitrary or authoritative.
E. Do not base your work on the power of position or of personality.
F. Permit and encourage the free expression of opinions.

III. Principle of Self-Growth

The success of the supervisor is measured by the extent to which, and the speed with which, he is no longer needed.

A. Base criticism on principles, not on specifics.
B. Point out higher activities to employees.
C. Train for self-thinking by employees to meet new situations.
D. Stimulate initiative, self-reliance, and individual responsibility
E. Concentrate on stimulating the growth of employees rather than on removing defects.

IV. Principle of Individual Worth

Respect for the individual is a paramount consideration in supervision.

A. Be human and sympathetic in dealing with employees.
B. Don't nag about things to be done.
C. Recognize the individual differences among employees and seek opportunities to permit best expression of each personality.

V. Principle of Creative Leadership

The best supervision is that which is not apparent to the employee.

A. Stimulate, don't drive employees to creative action.
B. Emphasize doing good things.
C. Encourage employees to do what they do best.
D. Do not be too greatly concerned with details of subject or method.
E. Do not be concerned exclusively with immediate problems and activities.
F. Reveal higher activities and make them both desired and maximally possible.
G. Determine procedures in the light of each situation but see that these are derived from a sound basic philosophy.
H. Aid, inspire, and lead so as to liberate the creative spirit latent in all good employees.

VI. Principle of Success and Failure

There are no unsuccessful employees, only unsuccessful supervisors who have failed to give proper leadership.

A. Adapt suggestions to the capacities, attitudes, and prejudices of employees.
B. Be gradual, be progressive, be persistent.
C. Help the employee find the general principle; have the employee apply his own problem to the general principle.
D. Give adequate appreciation for good work and honest effort.
E. Anticipate employee difficulties and help to prevent them.
F. Encourage employees to do the desirable things they will do anyway.
G. Judge your supervision by the results it secures.

VII. Principle of Science
Successful supervision is scientific, objective, and experimental. It is based on facts, not on prejudices.
A. Be cumulative in results.
B. Never divorce your suggestions from the goals of training.
C. Don't be impatient of results.
D. Keep all matters on a professional, not a personal, level.
E. Do not be concerned exclusively with immediate problems and activities.
F. Use objective means of determining achievement and rating where possible.

VIII. Principle of Cooperation
Supervision is a cooperative enterprise between supervisor and employee.
A. Begin with conditions as they are.
B. Ask opinions of all involved when formulating policies.
C. Organization is as good as its weakest link.
D. Let employees help to determine policies and department programs.
E. Be approachable and accessible—physically and mentally.
F. Develop pleasant social relationships.

WHAT IS ADMINISTRATION

Administration is concerned with providing the environment, the material facilities, and the operational procedures that will promote the maximum growth and development of supervisors and employees. (Organization is an aspect and a concomitant of administration.)

There is no sharp line of demarcation between supervision and administration; these functions are intimately interrelated and, often, overlapping. They are complementary activities.

I. Practices Commonly Classed as "Supervisory"
A. Conducting employees' conferences
B. Visiting sections, units, offices, divisions, departments
C. Arranging for demonstrations
D. Examining plans
E. Suggesting professional reading
F. Interpreting bulletins
G. Recommending in-service training courses
H. Encouraging experimentation
I. Appraising employee morale
J. Providing for intervisitation

II. Practices Commonly Classified as "Administrative"
A. Management of the office
B. Arrangement of schedules for extra duties
C. Assignment of rooms or areas
D. Distribution of supplies
E. Keeping records and reports
F. Care of audio-visual materials
G. Keeping inventory records
H. Checking record cards and books

I. Programming special activities
J. Checking on the attendance and punctuality of employees

III. Practices Commonly Classified as Both "Supervisory" and "Administrative"
  A. Program construction
  B. Testing or evaluating outcomes
  C. Personnel accounting
  D. Ordering instructional materials

RESPONSIBILITIES OF THE SUPERVISOR

A person employed in a supervisory capacity must constantly be able to improve his own efficiency and ability. He represent the employer to the employees and only continuous self-examination can make him a capable supervisor.

Leadership and training are the supervisor's responsibility. An efficient working unit is one in which the employees work with the supervisor. It is his job to bring out the best in his employees. He must always be relaxed, courteous, and calm in his association with his employees. Their feelings are important, and a harsh attitude does not develop the most efficient employees.

COMPETENCES OF THE SUPERVISOR

I. Complete knowledge of the duties and responsibilities of his position.
II. To be able to organize a job, plan ahead, and carry through.
III. To have self-confidence and initiative.
IV. To be able to handle the unexpected situation and make quick decisions.
V. To be able to properly train subordinates in the positions they are best suited for.
VI. To be able to keep good human relations among his subordinates.
VII. To be able to keep good human relations between his subordinates and himself and to earn their respect and trust.

THE PROFESSIONAL SUPERVISOR-EMPLOYEE RELATIONSHIP

There are two kinds of efficiency: one kind is only apparent and is produced in organizations through the exercise of mere discipline; this is but a simulation of the second, or true, efficiency which springs from spontaneous cooperation. If you are a manager, no matter how great or small your responsibility, it is your job, in the final analysis, to create and develop this involuntary cooperation among the people whom you supervise. For, no matter how powerful a combination of money, machines, and materials a company may have, this is a dead and sterile thing without a team of willing, thinking, and articulate people to guide it.

The following 21 points are presented as indicative of the exemplary basic relationship that should exist between supervisor and employee:

1. Each person wants to be liked and respected by his fellow employee and wants to be treated with consideration and respect by his superior.
2. The most competent employee will make an error. However, in a unit where good relations exist between the supervisor and his employees, tenseness and fear do not exist. Thus, errors are not hidden or covered up, and the efficiency of a unit is not impaired.

3. Subordinates resent rules, regulations, or orders that are unreasonable or unexplained.
4. Subordinates are quick to resent unfairness, harshness, injustices, and favoritism.
5. An employee will accept responsibility if he knows that he will be complimented for a job well done, and not too harshly chastised for failure; that his supervisor will check the cause of the failure, and, if it was the supervisor's fault, he will assume the blame therefore. If it was the employee's fault, his supervisor will explain the correct method or means of handling the responsibility.
6. An employee wants to receive credit for a suggestion he has made, that is used. If a suggestion cannot be used, the employee is entitled to an explanation. The supervisor should not say "no" and close the subject.
7. Fear and worry slow up a worker's ability. Poor working environment can impair his physical and mental health. A good supervisor avoids forceful methods, threats, and arguments to get a job done.
8. A forceful supervisor is able to train his employees individually and as a team, and is able to motivate them in the proper channels.
9. A mature supervisor is able to properly evaluate his subordinates and to keep them happy and satisfied.
10. A sensitive supervisor will never patronize his subordinates.
11. A worthy supervisor will respect his employees' confidences.
12. Definite and clear-cut responsibilities should be assigned to each executive.
13. Responsibility should always be coupled with corresponding authority.
14. No change should be made in the scope or responsibilities of a position without a definite understanding to that effect on the part of all persons concerned.
15. No executive or employee, occupying a single position in the organization, should be subject to definite orders from more than one source.
16. Orders should never be given to subordinates over the head of a responsible executive. Rather than do this, the officer in question should be supplanted.
17. Criticisms of subordinates should, whoever possible, be made privately, and in no case should a subordinate be criticized in the presence of executives or employees of equal or lower rank.
18. No dispute or difference between executives or employees as to authority or responsibilities should be considered too trivial for prompt and careful adjudication.
19. Promotions, wage changes, and disciplinary action should always be approved by the executive immediately superior to the one directly responsible.
20. No executive or employee should ever be required, or expected, to be at the same time an assistant to, and critic of, another.
21. Any executive whose work is subject to regular inspection should, wherever practicable, be given the assistance and facilities necessary to enable him to maintain an independent check of the quality of his work.

MINI-TEXT IN SUPERVISION, ADMINISTRATION, MANAGEMENT, AND ORGANIZATION

I. Brief Highlights

Listed concisely and sequentially are major headings and important data in the field for quick recall and review.

A. Levels of Management

Any organization of some size has several levels of management. In terms of a ladder, the levels are:

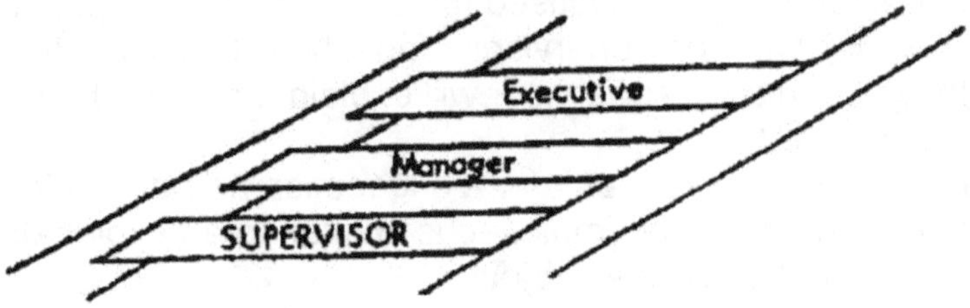

The first level is very important because it is the beginning point of management leadership.

B. What the Supervisor Must Learn

A supervisor must learn to:

1. Deal with people and their differences
2. Get the job done through people
3. Recognize the problems when they exist
4. Overcome obstacles to good performance
5. Evaluate the performance of people
6. Check his own performance in terms of accomplishment

C. A Definition of Supervisor

The term supervisor means any individual having authority, in the interests of the employer, to hire, transfer, suspend, lay-off, recall, promote, discharge, assign, reward, or discipline other employees or responsibility to direct them, or to adjust their grievances, or effectively to recommend such action, if, in connection with the foregoing, exercise of such authority is not of a merely routine or clerical nature but requires the use of independent judgment.

D. Elements of the Team Concept

What is involved in teamwork? The component parts are:

1. Members
2. A leader
3. Goals
4. Plans
5. Cooperation
6. Spirit

E. Principles of Organization

1. A team member must know what his job is.
2. Be sure that the nature and scope of a job are understood.
3. Authority and responsibility should be carefully spelled out.
4. A supervisor should be permitted to make the maximum number of decisions affecting his employees.
5. Employees should report to only one supervisor.
6. A supervisor should direct only as many employees as he can handle effectively.
7. An organization plan should be flexible.

8. Inspection and performance of work should be separate.
9. Organizational problems should receive immediate attention.
10. Assign work in line with ability and experience.

F. The Four Important Parts of Every Job
1. Inherent in every job is the *accountability* for results.
2. A second set of factors in every job is *responsibilities*.
3. Along with duties and responsibilities one must have the *authority* to act within certain limits without obtaining permission to proceed.
4. No job exists in a vacuum. The supervisor is surrounded by key *relationships*.

G. Principles of Delegation
Where work is delegated for the first time, the supervisor should think in terms of these questions:
1. Who is best qualified to do this?
2. Can an employee improve his abilities by doing this?
3. How long should an employee spend on this?
4. Are there any special problems for which he will need guidance?
5. How broad a delegation can I make?

H. Principles of Effective Communications
1. Determine the media.
2. To whom directed?
3. Identification and source authority.
4. Is communication understood?

I. Principles of Work Improvement
1. Most people usually do only the work which is assigned to them.
2. Workers are likely to fit assigned work into the time available to perform it.
3. A good workload usually stimulates output.
4. People usually do their best work when they know that results will be reviewed or inspected.
5. Employees usually feel that someone else is responsible for conditions of work, workplace layout, job methods, type of tools/equipment, and other such factors.
6. Employees are usually defensive about their job security.
7. Employees have natural resistance to change.
8. Employees can support or destroy a supervisor.
9. A supervisor usually earns the respect of his people through his personal example of diligence and efficiency.

J. Areas of Job Improvement
The areas of job improvement are quite numerous, but the most common ones which a supervisor can identify and utilize are:
1. Departmental layout
2. Flow of work
3. Workplace layout
4. Utilization of manpower
5. Work methods
6. Materials handling

7. Utilization
8. Motion economy

K. Seven Key Points in Making Improvements
1. Select the job to be improved
2. Study how it is being done now
3. Question the present method
4. Determine actions to be taken
5. Chart proposed method
6. Get approval and apply
7. Solicit worker participation

I. Corrective Techniques of Job Improvement

Specific Problems
1. Size of workload
2. Inability to meet schedules
3. Strain and fatigue
4. Improper use of men and skills
5. Waste, poor quality, unsafe conditions
6. Bottleneck conditions that hinder output
7. Poor utilization of equipment and machine
8. Efficiency and productivity of labor

General Improvement
1. Departmental layout
2. Flow of work
3. Work plan layout
4. Utilization of manpower
5. Work methods
6. Materials handling
7. Utilization of equipment
8. Motion economy

Corrective Techniques
1. Study with scale model
2. Flow chart study
3. Motion analysis
4. Comparison of units produced to standard allowance
5. Methods analysis
6. Flow chart and equipment study
7. Down time vs. running time
8. Motion analysis

M. A Planning Checklist
1. Objectives
2. Controls
3. Delegations
4. Communications
5. Resources
6. Manpower

7. Equipment
8. Supplies and materials
9. Utilization of time
10. Safety
11. Money
12. Work
13. Timing of improvements

N. Five Characteristics of Good Directions
In order to get results, directions must be:
1. Possible of accomplishment
2. Agreeable with worker interests
3. Related to mission
4. Planned and complete
5. Unmistakably clear

O. Types of Directions
1. Demands or direct orders
2. Requests
3. Suggestion or implication
4. volunteering

P. Controls
A typical listing of the overall areas in which the supervisor should establish controls might be:
1. Manpower
2. Materials
3. Quality of work
4. Quantity of work
5. Time
6. Space
7. Money
8. Methods

Q. Orienting the New Employee
1. Prepare for him
2. Welcome the new employee
3. Orientation for the job
4. Follow-up

R. Checklist for Orienting New Employees

	Yes	No
1. Do you appreciate the feelings of new employees when they first report for work?	___	___
2. Are you aware of the fact that the new employee must make a big adjustment to his job?	___	___
3. Have you given him good reasons for liking the job and the organization?	___	___
4. Have you prepared for his first day on the job?	___	___
5. Did you welcome him cordially and make him feel needed?	___	___

		Yes	No
6.	Did you establish rapport with him so that he feels free to talk and discuss matters with you?	___	___
7.	Did you explain his job to him and his relationship to you?	___	___
8.	Does he know that his work will be evaluated periodically on a basis that is fair and objective?	___	___
9.	Did you introduce him to his fellow workers in such a way that they are likely to accept him?	___	___
10.	Does he know what employee benefits he will receive?	___	___
11.	Does he understand the importance of being on the job and what to do if he must leave his duty station?	___	___
12.	Has he been impressed with the importance of accident prevention and safe practice?	___	___
13.	Does he generally know his way around the department?	___	___
14.	Is he under the guidance of a sponsor who will teach the right way of doing things?	___	___
15.	Do you plan to follow-up so that he will continue to adjust successfully to his job?	___	___

S. Principles of Learning
1. Motivation
2. Demonstration or explanation
3. Practice

T. Causes of Poor Performance
1. Improper training for job
2. Wrong tools
3. Inadequate directions
4. Lack of supervisory follow-up
5. Poor communications
6. Lack of standards of performance
7. Wrong work habits
8. Low morale
9. Other

U. Four Major Steps in On-The-Job Instruction
1. Prepare the worker
2. Present the operation
3. Tryout performance
4. Follow-up

V. Employees Want Five Things
1. Security
2. Opportunity
3. Recognition
4. Inclusion
5. Expression

W. Some Don'ts in Regard to Praise
1. Don't praise a person for something he hasn't done.
2. Don't praise a person unless you can be sincere.
3. Don't be sparing in praise just because your superior withholds it from you.
4. Don't let too much time elapse between good performance and recognition of it

X. How to Gain Your Workers' Confidence

Methods of developing confidence include such things as:
1. Knowing the interests, habits, hobbies of employees
2. Admitting your own inadequacies
3. Sharing and telling of confidence in others
4. Supporting people when they are in trouble
5. Delegating matters that can be well handled
6. Being frank and straightforward about problems and working conditions
7. Encouraging others to bring their problems to you
8. Taking action on problems which impede worker progress

Y. Sources of Employee Problems

On-the-job causes might be such things as:
1. A feeling that favoritism is exercised in assignments
2. Assignment of overtime
3. An undue amount of supervision
4. Changing methods or systems
5. Stealing of ideas or trade secrets
6. Lack of interest in job
7. Threat of reduction in force
8. Ignorance or lack of communications
9. Poor equipment
10. Lack of knowing how supervisor feels toward employee
11. Shift assignments

Off-the-job problems might have to do with:
1. Health
2. Finances
3. Housing
4. Family

Z. The Supervisor's Key to Discipline

There are several key points about discipline which the supervisor should keep in mind:
1. Job discipline is one of the disciplines of life and is directed by the supervisor.
2. It is more important to correct an employee fault than to fix blame for it.
3. Employee performance is affected by problems both on the job and off.
4. Sudden or abrupt changes in behavior can be indications of important employee problems.
5. Problems should be dealt with as soon as possible after they are identified.
6. The attitude of the supervisor may have more to do with solving problems than the techniques of problem solving.
7. Correction of employee behavior should be resorted to only after the supervisor is sure that training or counseling will not be helpful.

8. Be sure to document your disciplinary actions.
9. Make sure that you are disciplining on the basis of facts rather than personal feelings.
10. Take each disciplinary step in order, being careful not to make snap judgments, or decisions based on impatience.

AA. Five Important Processes of Management

1. Planning
2. Organizing
3. Scheduling
4. Controlling
5. Motivating

BB. When the Supervisor Fails to Plan

1. Supervisor creates impression of not knowing his job
2. May lead to excessive overtime
3. Job runs itself—supervisor lacks control
4. Deadlines and appointments missed
5. Parts of the work go undone
6. Work interrupted by emergencies
7. Sets a bad example
8. Uneven workload creates peaks and valleys
9. Too much time on minor details at expense of more important tasks

CC. Fourteen General Principles of Management

1. Division of work
2. Authority and responsibility
3. Discipline
4. Unity of command
5. Unity of direction
6. Subordination of individual interest to general interest
7. Remuneration of personnel
8. Centralization
9. Scalar chain
10. Order
11. Equity
12. Stability of tenure of personnel
13. Initiative
14. Esprit de corps

DD. Change

Bringing about change is perhaps attempted more often, and yet less well understood, than anything else the supervisor does. How do people generally react to change? (People tend to resist change that is imposed upon them by other individuals or circumstances.

Change is characteristic of every situation. It is a part of every real endeavor where the efforts of people are concerned.

1. Why do people resist change?
   People may resist change because of:
   a. Fear of the unknown
   b. Implied criticism
   c. Unpleasant experiences in the past
   d. Fear of loss of status
   e. Threat to the ego
   f. Fear of loss of economic stability

2. How can we best overcome the resistance to change?
   In initiating change, take these steps:
   a. Get ready to sell
   b. Identify sources of help
   c. Anticipate objections
   d. Sell benefits
   e. Listen in depth
   f. Follow up

II. Brief Topical Summaries

A. Who/What is the Supervisor?
1. The supervisor is often called the "highest level employee and the lowest level manager."
2. A supervisor is a member of both management and the work group. He acts as a bridge between the two.
3. Most problems in supervision are in the area of human relations, or people problems.
4. Employees expect: Respect, opportunity to learn and to advance, and a sense of belonging, and so forth.
5. Supervisors are responsible for directing people and organizing work. Planning is of paramount importance.
6. A position description is a set of duties and responsibilities inherent to a given position.
7. It is important to keep the position description up-to-date and to provide each employee with his own copy.

B. The Sociology of Work
1. People are alike in many ways; however, each individual is unique.
2. The supervisor is challenged in getting to know employee differences. Acquiring skills in evaluating individuals is an asset.
3. Maintaining meaningful working relationships in the organization is of great importance.
4. The supervisor has an obligation to help individuals to develop to their fullest potential.
5. Job rotation on a planned basis helps to build versatility and to maintain interest and enthusiasm in work groups.
6. Cross training (job rotation) provides backup skills.

7. The supervisor can help reduce tension by maintaining a sense of humor, providing guidance to employees, and by making reasonable and timely decisions. Employees respond favorably to working under reasonably predictable circumstances.
8. Change is characteristic of all managerial behavior. The supervisor must adjust to changes in procedures, new methods, technological changes, and to a number of new and sometimes challenging situations.
9. To overcome the natural tendency for people to resist change, the supervisor should become more skillful in initiating change.

C. Principles and Practices of Supervision

1. Employees should be required to answer to only one superior.
2. A supervisor can effectively direct only a limited number of employees, depending upon the complexity, variety, and proximity of the jobs involved.
3. The organizational chart presents the organization in graphic form. It reflects lines of authority and responsibility as well as interrelationships of units within the organization.
4. Distribution of work can be improved through an analysis using the "Work Distribution Chart."
5. The "Work Distribution Chart" reflects the division of work within a unit in understandable form.
6. When related tasks are given to an employee, he has a better chance of increasing his skills through training.
7. The individual who is given the responsibility for tasks must also be given the appropriate authority to insure adequate results.
8. The supervisor should delegate repetitive, routine work. Preparation of recurring reports, maintaining leave and attendance records are some examples.
9. Good discipline is essential to good task performance. Discipline is reflected in the actions of employees on the job in the absence of supervision.
10. Disciplinary action may have to be taken when the positive aspects of discipline have failed. Reprimand, warning, and suspension are examples of disciplinary action.
11. If a situation calls for a reprimand, be sure it is deserved and remember it is to be done in private.

D. Dynamic Leadership

1. A style is a personal method or manner of exerting influence.
2. Authoritarian leaders often see themselves as the source of power and authority.
3. The democratic leader often perceives the group as the source of authority and power.
4. Supervisors tend to do better when using the pattern of leadership that is most natural for them.
5. Social scientists suggest that the effective supervisor use the leadership style that best fits the problem or circumstances involved.
6. All four styles—telling, selling, consulting, joining—have their place. Using one does not preclude using the other at another time.

7. The theory X point of view assumes that the average person dislikes work, will avoid it whenever possible, and must be coerced to achieve organizational objectives.
8. The theory Y point of view assumes that the average person considers work to be a natural as play, and, when the individual is committed, he requires little supervision or direction to accomplish desired objectives.
9. The leader's basic assumptions concerning human behavior and human nature affect his actions, decisions, and other managerial practices.
10. Dissatisfaction among employees is often present, but difficult to isolate. The supervisor should seek to weaken dissatisfaction by keeping promises, being sincere and considerate, keeping employees informed, and so forth.
11. Constructive suggestions should be encouraged during the natural progress of the work.

E. Processes for Solving Problems

1. People find their daily tasks more meaningful and satisfying when they can improve them.
2. The causes of problems, or the key factors, are often hidden in the background. Ability to solve problems often involves the ability to isolate them from their backgrounds. There is some substance to the cliché that some persons "can't see the forest for the trees."
3. New procedures are often developed from old ones. Problems should be broken down into manageable parts. New ideas can be adapted from old one.
4. People think differently in problem-solving situations. Using a logical, patterned approach is often useful. One approach found to be useful includes these steps:
    a. Define the problem
    b. Establish objectives
    c. Get the facts
    d. Weigh and decide
    e. Take action
    f. Evaluate action

F. Training for Results

1. Participants respond best when they feel training is important to them.
2. The supervisor has responsibility for the training and development of those who report to him.
3. When training is delegated to others, great care must be exercised to insure the trainer has knowledge, aptitude, and interest for his work as a trainer.
4. Training (learning) of some type goes on continually. The most successful supervisor makes certain the learning contributes in a productive manner to operational goals.
5. New employees are particularly susceptible to training. Older employees facing new job situations require specific training, as well as having need for development and growth opportunities.
6. Training needs require continuous monitoring.
7. The training officer of an agency is a professional with a responsibility to assist supervisors in solving training problems.

8. Many of the self-development steps important to the supervisor's own growth are equally important to the development of peers and subordinates. Knowledge of these is important when the supervisor consults with others on development and growth opportunities.

G. Health, Safety, and Accident Prevention

1. Management-minded supervisors take appropriate measures to assist employees in maintaining health and in assuring safe practices in the work environment.
2. Effective safety training and practices help to avoid injury and accidents.
3. Safety should be a management goal. All infractions of safety which are observed should be corrected without exception.
4. Employees' safety attitude, training and instruction, provision of safe tools and equipment, supervision, and leadership are considered highly important factors which contribute to safety and which can be influenced directly by supervisors.
5. When accidents do occur, they should be investigated promptly for very important reasons, including the fact that information which is gained can be used to prevent accidents in the future.

H. Equal Employment Opportunity

1. The supervisor should endeavor to treat all employees fairly, without regard to religion, race, sex, or national origin.
2. Groups tend to reflect the attitude of the leader. Prejudice can be detected even in very subtle form. Supervisors must strive to create a feeling of mutual respect and confidence in every employee.
3. Complete utilization of all human resources is a national goal. Equitable consideration should be accorded women in the work force, minority-group members, the physically and mentally handicapped, and the older employee. The important question is: "Who can do the job?"
4. Training opportunities, recognition for performance, overtime assignments, promotional opportunities, and all other personnel actions are to be handled on an equitable basis.

I. Improving Communications

1. Communications is achieving understanding between the sender and the receiver of a message. It also means sharing information—the creation of understanding.
2. Communication is basic to all human activity. Words are means of conveying meanings; however, real meanings are in people.
3. There are very practical differences in the effectiveness of one-way, impersonal, and two-way communications. Words spoken face-to-face are better understood. Telephone conversations are effective, but lack the rapport of person-to-person exchanges. The whole person communicates.
4. Cooperation and communication in an organization go hand in hand. When there is a mutual respect between people, spelling out rules and procedures for communicating is unnecessary.
5. There are several barriers to effective communications. These include failure to listen with respect and understanding, lack of skill in feedback, and misinterpreting the meanings of words used by the speaker. It is also common

practice to listen to what we want to hear, and tune out things we do not want to hear.

6. Communication is management's chief problem. The supervisor should accept the challenge to communicate more effectively and to improve interagency and intra-agency communications.
7. The supervisor may often plan for and conduct meetings. The planning phase is critical and may determine the success or the failure of a meeting.
8. Speaking before groups usually requires extra effort. Stage fright may never disappear completely, but it can be controlled.

J. Self-Development

1. Every employee is responsible for his own self-development.
2. Toastmaster and toastmistress clubs offer opportunities to improve skills in oral communications.
3. Planning for one's own self-development is of vital importance. Supervisors know their own strengths and limitations better than anyone else.
4. Many opportunities are open to aid the supervisor in his developmental efforts, including job assignments; training opportunities, both governmental and non-governmental—to include universities and professional conferences and seminars.
5. Programmed instruction offers a means of studying at one's own rate.
6. Where difficulties may arise from a supervisor's being away from his work for training, he may participate in televised home study or correspondence courses to meet his self-development needs.

K. Teaching and Training

1. The Teaching Process

Teaching is encouraging and guiding the learning activities of students toward established goals. In most cases this process consists of five steps: preparation, presentation, summarization, evaluation, and application.

a. Preparation

Preparation is two-fold in nature; that of the supervisor and the employee. Preparation by the supervisor is absolutely essential to success. He must know what, when, where, how, and whom he will teach. Some of the factors that should be considered are:

1) The objectives
2) The materials needed
3) The methods to be used
4) Employee participation
5) Employee interest
6) Training aids
7) Evaluation
8) Summarization

Employee preparation consists in preparing the employee to receive the material. Probably the most important single factor in the preparation of the employee is arousing and maintaining his interest. He must know the objectives of the training, why he is there, how the material can be used, and its importance to him.

b. Presentation
In presentation, have a carefully designed plan and follow it. The plan should be accurate and complete, yet flexible enough to meet situations as they arise. The method of presentation will be determined by the particular situation and objectives.

c. Summary
A summary should be made at the end of every training unit and program. In addition, there may be internal summaries depending on the nature of the material being taught. The important thing is that the trainee must always be able to understand how each part of the new material relates to the whole.

d. Application
The supervisor must arrange work so the employee will be given a chance to apply new knowledge or skills while the material is still clear in his mind and interest is high. The trainee does not really know whether he has learned the material until he has been given a chance to apply it. If the material is not applied, it loses most of its value.

e. Evaluation
The purpose of all training is to promote learning. To determine whether the training has been a success or failure, the supervisor must evaluate this learning.
In the broadest sense, evaluation includes all the devices, methods, skills, and techniques used by the supervisor to keep himself and the employees informed as to their progress toward the objectives they are pursuing. The extent to which the employee has mastered the knowledge, skills, and abilities, or changed his attitudes, as determined by the program objectives, is the extent to which instruction has succeeded or failed.
Evaluation should not be confined to the end of the lesson, day, or program but should be used continuously. We shall note later the way this relates to the rest of the teaching process.

2. Teaching Methods
A teaching method is a pattern of identifiable student and instructor activity used in presenting training material.
All supervisors are faced with the problem of deciding which method should be used at a given time.

a. Lecture
The lecture is direct oral presentation of material by the supervisor. The present trend is to place less emphasis on the trainer's activity and more on that of the trainee.

b. Discussion
Teaching by discussion or conference involves using questions and other techniques to arouse interest and focus attention upon certain areas, and by doing so creating a learning situation. This can be one of the most

valuable methods because it gives the employees an opportunity to express their ideas and pool their knowledge.

c. Demonstration
The demonstration is used to teach how something works or how to do something. It can be used to show a principle or what the results of a series of actions will be. A well-staged demonstration is particularly effective because it shows proper methods of performance in a realistic manner.

d. Performance
Performance is one of the most fundamental of all learning techniques or teaching methods. The trainee may be able to tell how a specific operation should be performed but he cannot be sure he knows how to perform the operation until he has done so.
As with all methods, there are certain advantages and disadvantages to each method.

e. Which Method to Use
Moreover, there are other methods and techniques of teaching. It is difficult to use any method without other methods entering into it. In any learning situation, a combination of methods is usually more effective than any one method alone.

Finally, evaluation must be integrated into the other aspects of the teaching-learning process.

It must be used in the motivation of the trainees; it must be used to assist in developing understanding during the training; and it must be related to employee application of the results of training.

This is distinctly the role of the supervisor.

PAYROLL NOTES & RESOURCES

PAYROLL PRINCIPLES

The maintenance of payroll records, processing of payroll changes, and the preparation of payroll registers, salary checks, and related reports are accomplished by the use of electronic equipment or manual methods. All payrolls covering State employees are computer processed, except where it is determined to be impractical. Payrolls are controlled on a change basis. Except for automated actions, changes to the previous payroll are required to be reported by the agencies on prescribed forms. There are two types of payrolls which are computer processed. The first is the *main* or *regular* payroll. Main payrolls and *special* payrolls are assigned to separate processing schedules, and due dates for submission of payroll forms are established accordingly.

Main payrolls are the normal state payrolls processed on the regular biweekly schedule. It is characteristic of such payrolls that they are in the process of being prepared during the period in which the employee is earning the money. All employees are paid on a main payroll unless specifically assigned to a special payroll. Special payrolls are to be established only on the basis of specific instructions from the Department of Audit and Control. Special payrolls have certain characteristics:

a. They may be hourly or per diem payrolls where steps to initiate payment are taken by the payroll agency only after work has been completed or substantially performed.
b. They may be payrolls involving temporary employees.
c. They may be *one-time* payrolls where the employee is paid at the completion of some specific task.

The following payroll change actions are automated for agency payrolls:

a. All employees on an annual or biweekly pay basis who receive other than a normal biweekly gross payment in the following pay period. Agencies are not required to submit forms for this change.
b. All employees paid on an hourly or daily rate or fee basis are reduced to a zero amount after each payment. Unless a PR-75 (a form which would change their status) is submitted in the following period, they are not paid.
c. All employees reported as being separated from service within the pay period, and who receive payment for part of the pay period, are released from the payroll the following period. A form for removal need not be submitted.
d. All employees restored to the payroll for the sole purpose of lump sum payment of leave accruals or any type of adjustment are released from the payroll the following period. A form for removal need not be submitted.

Special payrolls may be an exception. Some special payrolls are not normalized; the employee receives the same payment as in the previous period unless a PR-75 is submitted.

The Department of Audit and Control is responsible for the accounting, control, and reporting of deductions for payrolls processed by the Department.

Payroll Forms

The following major forms are used by payroll agencies for reporting the information required in the payroll process.

a. Payroll and Personnel Transaction Form
b. Transmittal Form Payroll/Personnel Transactions and Payroll Certification
c. Payroll Deduction Form
d. Transmittal for Payroll Deduction Forms
e. Payroll Header File Change Notice
f. Report of Check Returned for Refund or Exchange

Basic Payroll Information

The payroll agency code, assigned by Audit and Control, is made up of a two-digit department code and a three-digit division or institution code. The five digits in combination represent the payroll agency code. These identification codes are shown on all papers submitted in relation to the payroll process, including forms requesting the release, refund, or exchange of salary checks. Payroll periods are numbered consecutively within the fiscal year from 1 to 26 (or 27). Payroll period numbers are indicated on the payday calendar, prepared and distributed annually by the Department of Audit and Control.

A line item number is used to identify each position in the payroll agency. All line numbers for computer processed payrolls appear on the payroll register as five-digit numbers. If an employee is to be paid from two or more line items during a payroll period, the employee will appear on the payroll in the most recent item only. The employee's gross salary will represent the total amount paid from both items. If this gross salary is payable from items in different appropriations, an adjustment will be made by the Department of Audit and Control on the computer-prepared Appropriations Charge Sheet, based on the split charge information reported on *Payroll and Personnel Transaction Form* by the agency.

Because of the timing and scheduling requirements involved in the processing of payrolls, certain deadlines or due dates have been established for the submission of the required forms to the Departments of Audit and Control and Civil Service. These due dates must be rigidly adhered to. Any payroll or personnel transaction not accomplished in time for submission by the specified due date must be held in the payroll agency for processing with the payroll data for the next payroll period. Payroll agencies will serve their own best interests by establishing strong internal controls and procedures to assure the complete and timely processing of payroll information. In setting forth the due dates, it is to be understood that DAY 1 is the first day of the payroll period (Thursday), and DAY 14 is the last (Wednesday). Intervening days are numbered in sequence.

Payroll and Personnel Transaction Forms

The purpose of the Form is three-fold:

a. To advise the Department of Audit and Control of changes to be made affecting payroll preparation in terms of adding, changing, or deleting data, and to provide necessary related information.
b. To provide the Department of Civil Service with information to be used in certification, re-certification, and record keeping.

c. To provide the payroll agency with a record of the basic data concerning payroll and personnel transactions, and to provide a control for further processing of such transactions.

Payroll and Personnel Transaction Forms are submitted to the Departments of Civil Service and Audit and Control under the Transmittal Form.

These are generally separated into three groups. The general rule of thumb is as follows:

Group I - Appointments, Line Changes, or anything involving a title or status change, three parts go to Civil Service. Civil Service approves or disapproves them and sends 1 part to Audit and Control and 1 part is kept by the agency.

Group II - Separations of any type or changes to employee basic information such as name. 1 part to Audit and Control, 1 part to Civil Service, 3 parts kept by the agency.

Group III - Changes in salary or biweekly pay. 1 part sent to Audit and Control, 4 parts kept by the agency.

When an employee leaves state service after being off the payroll for 2 full biweekly pay periods or 4 weeks, they may receive payment for their accrued vacation and overtime not in excess of 30 days each. The only two times they may be immediately paid this lump sum is if they retire or are laid off.

Inconvenience pay is additional compensation over an employee's basic salary which is authorized for employees who are required to work four or more hours between 6:00 P.M. and 6:00 A.M. in their regular tour of duty. Hours worked between 6:00 P.M. and 6:00 A.M. on an overtime basis are not included when determining eligibility for inconvenience pay.

Location pay is additional compensation granted to an employee whose principal place of employment or official station is located in certain parts of the state.

A reallocation is a change in the grade of an existing title with no change in the title.

A reclassification is a change in an existing title. The new title may retain the same salary grade or be allocated to a lower or higher salary grade.

There is an *Index to Transaction Codes for the Classified Service* that is available to assist payroll offices. For example, listed below are some of the codes and what they represent. It is not necessary to memorize them.

	Group I
PREF	Preferred List Appointment
CERT	Recertificat ion
GLASS	Reclassification
PROB COMP	Successful Completion of Probationary Period

	Group II
RETIRED	Retirement
SICK LV	Sick leave of absence without pay or with half pay
TERM LV	Termination of leave - probationary period completed in another agency
MIL LV	Military leave without pay

	Group III
OT INC SF	Overtime including intermittent inconvenienc and partial shift pay
PRM OT	Premium Overtime
STANDBY	Payment for standby-on-call

Salary and Calculation Data

Many of the questions on this section of the exam have traditionally involved calculating salaries. We have provided information on how this is actually done in state payroll departments. This information should be very helpful to you, if you practice using it. We suggest you make up your own possible test questions as well as doing the practice questions we have provided. (One note of caution: The factors and formulas listed below are the actual, real-life formulas. Often on exams, they will give you other factors and formulas to work with. People who actually work in payroll sometimes lose points because they use the actual factors, instead of those given on the exam. Remember, this is an exam, not real-life, so you should work with what is given to you.

Factors and Formulas for the Calculation of Wages

The following factors and formulas are used to compute wages due annual salaried employees.

ANNUAL

a. Pay basis code ANN (10-day basis)
Annual salaried employees paid on a biweekly basis over the full calendar year.

365-Day Year
Biweekly Rate = .038356 x annual salary
Work Day Rate = .10 x biweekly rate

366-Day Year
Biweekly Rate = .038251 x annual salary
Work Day Rate = .10 x biweekly rate

NOTE: An exception: State University professional staff paid on an annual (ANN) basis. For these employees, use the 14-day calendar basis for general increases and discretionary increases effective July first when salary due for the period is paid at two different rates. (See CAL pay basis code for 14 day factors.) You shouldn't need to know this for the exam.

b. Pay basis code 8AN (8-day basis)
Annual salaried employees paid for 8 days in a biweekly period (10-hour day).

365-Day Year
Biweekly Rate = .038356 x annual salary
Work Day Rate = .125 x biweekly rate

366-Day Year
Biweekly Rate = .038251 x annual salary
Work Day Rate = .125 x biweekly rate

10 MONTH

Pay basis code 10M (10-day basis)
Annual salaried employees paid on a biweekly basis over a 10 month period.

365-Day Year
Biweekly Rate = .046204 x annual salary
Work Day Rate = .10 x biweekly rate

366-Day Year
Biweekly Rate = .046052 x annual salary
Work Day Rate = .10 x biweekly rate

NOTE: An exception: 10-month employees are paid on the following 14-day calendar basis during the first and the last payroll periods of school year.

365-Day Year and 366-Day Year
Calendar Day Rate = .0714286 x biweekly rate

21 PERIOD or COLLEGE YEAR-PART

Pay basis code 21P or CYP (14-day basis)
Annual salaried employees paid on a biweekly basis over 21 biweekly pay periods.

21 Periods
Biweekly Rate = .047619 x annual salary
Calendar Day Rate = .0714286 x biweekly rate

CALENDAR or COLLEGE YEAR-FULL

Pay basis code CAL or CYF (14-day basis)
Annual salaried employees paid on a biweekly basis over the full calendar year.

365-Day Year
Biweekly Rate = .038356 x annual salary
Calendar Day Rate = .0714286 x biweekly rate

366-Day Year
Biweekly Rate = .038356 x annual salary
Calendar Day Rate = .0714286 x biweekly rate

Calculation of Wages

The following prescribed methods and formulas MUST be used in calculating wages due. In all instances, mills must be dropped after each separate calculation.

ADDITIONAL SALARY FACTORS	When applying additional salary factors such as location pay, inconvenience pay, geographic and shift differentials, premium overtime, and premium holiday, add the annual amount of additional payment to basic annual salary. Multiply the total annual by the biweekly factor to obtain the biweekly rate. If preshift briefing pay is also applicable, add this amount to the biweekly rate.
BIWEEKLY RATE	Total annual salary x biweekly factor = biweekly rate
WORK DAY RATE	Pay basis codes *ANN, *10M, and BIW are processed as having 10 work days in a biweekly period. The work day rate is 1/10 of the biweekly rate. Biweekly rate x .10 = work day rate *An exception is made for pay basis codes ANN for State University professional staff and 10M during the first and last payroll periods of the school year. All those times the 14 day calendar rate is used (biweekly rate x .0714286). Pay basis code 8AN processed as having a 10-hour work day, 4 days per week. The work day rate is 1/8 of the biweekly rate. Biweekly rate x .125 = work day rate Pay basis codes 14D, CAL, 21P, CYF, CYP, and SES are processed on a 14-day biweekly basis. The calendar day rate is 1/14 of the biweekly rate. Biweekly rate x .0714286 = calendar day rate
LOST TIME AMOUNT	The amount to be deducted from biweekly wages for lost time is calculated as follows: Work day rate x number of days lost = lost time amount
OVERTIME RATE	Payment for overtime service (hours worked in excess of 40 hours in any work week) is made at one and one-half times the hourly rate of pay for the position in which the overtime is rendered. The overtime compensation rate is determined as follows:

Pay Basis
ANN, 8AN

Annual Salary	x	.00075		= 1 1/2 hourly rate
BIW Biweekly Rate	x	.0125	x 1.5	= 1 1/2 hourly rate
DLY Daily Rate	x	.125	x 1.5	= 1 1/2 hourly rate
HRY Hourly Rate	x		1.5	= 1 1/2 hourly rate

EXTRA SERVICE RATE	A. Payment due for extra service is determined in the same manner as for overtime, except that a straight hourly rate is paid for any hours required to bring the total work week to the 40-hour basis. The straight time extra service rate is determined as follows: Pay Basis ANN (Annual Salary) x .0005 = Straight Hourly Rate B. When the Extra Service Rate is fixed by the Director of the Budget , the payment due is calculated at the hourly rate shown on the Budget Certificate.
HOLIDAY PAY	Holiday compensation is calculated at the rate of one-tenth of the employee's biweekly rate of compensation for each full day of holiday work and includes appropriate additional salary factors (Pre-shift briefing pay is NOT allowed). Holiday compensation for less than a full day is prorated. For a full day Biweekly Rate x .10 = Holiday Pay Amount For a partial day Work Day Rate x Decimal Equivalent = Holiday Pay Amount
LUMP SUM PAYMENT	Lump sum payment due for accrued credits is calculated as follows: Work Day Rate x Number of days of accrued credits = Payment due Number of days for lump sum payment is always reported in full days, for both full-time and part-time employees.
PART-TIME INCUMBENTS of FULL-TIME POSITIONS	For part-time employees in full-time positions, the full annual salary and percentage of time worked are reported. The following formulas are used to calculate biweekly salary: Full Biweekly Rate = Annual salary x Biweekly factor Biweekly Payment = Full Biweekly Rate x Percent of Time Worked
INSTITUTION TEACHERS - ADDITIONAL COMPENSATION	Payment for incumbent Institution Teachers required to perform services during July and August is at an hourly rate, determined as follows: a. For services performed in a teaching title normally paid at a 1-month rate, Hourly Rate = Annual Salary ÷ 1736

b. For services performed in a position normally paid at a 12 month rate, Hourly Rate = Annual Salary ÷ 2000

Services paid may not exceed 40 hours in any one week.

DECIMAL EQUIVALENTS OF PARTS OF AN HOUR	
Hours	
1/4	= .25
1/2	= .50
3/4	= .75
1	= *1
*1 unit is an hour	

Payroll Deductions

All employee salary deductions as well as employee address and retirement system information, except as noted below, are controlled by the payroll agency. Whenever a payroll deduction is initiated, cancelled, or altered, the agency is responsible for submitting the appropriate information to the Department of Audit and Control on the Payroll Deduction Form.

Some deductions are not handled directly by most agencies. These, like garnishees, court orders, State Health Insurance, union dues are handled by Audit and Control, sometimes with assistance from the Department of Civil Service.

Deductions Greater Than Gross Salary

When an employee's gross salary is adjusted to less than normal by submission of a transaction form, any deduction based on a percentage rate (retirement contributions, social security, and withholding tax) is reduced automatically. The employee's net check must be greater than zero, or a check will not be processed. If, after percentage deductions are taken, the employee's gross salary is insufficient to cover all fixed deductions, some or all of these deductions are cancelled automatically in the following order of precedence:

1. Bonds
2. Retirement Loans
3. Federated Funds
4. Credit Union
5. Credit Union
6. Organization Dues
7. Taxable Maintenance
8. Non-taxable Maintenance
9. Automobile & Homeowners Insurance
10. General Insurance
11. TIAA Life
12. State Health Adjustment
13. State Health Insurance
14. Garnishee
15. Court Order
16. Fixed Federal Tax
17. Fixed State Tax
18. Fixed City Tax
19. Fines
20. Social Security Adjustment
21. Social Security Deficiency
22. Retirement Arrears

These deductions are resumed automatically when the employee's gross salary (after percentage deductions) is sufficient to cover them.

If the employee elects to cancel deductions in an order differing from that listed above, a form is prepared, indicating the deductions to be cancelled. When the employee's salary returns to normal, another form restoring and adjusting deductions as necessary is prepared. It is not necessary to adjust deductions for retirement loans or arrears.

www.ingramcontent.com/pod-product-compliance
Lightning Source LLC
Chambersburg PA
CBHW082040300426
44117CB00015B/2551
* 9 7 8 1 7 9 9 3 3 1 5 4 4 *